Traditional Recipes

D0302131

Publisher & Creative Director: Nick Wells
Senior Project Editor: Cat Emslie
Art Director: Mike Spender
Digital Design & Production: Chris Herbert

This is a **FLAME TREE** Book

FLAME TREE PUBLISHING
Crabtree Hall, Crabtree Lane
Fulham, London SW6 6TY
United Kingdom
www.flametreepublishing.com

Flame Tree is part of The Foundry Creative Media Company Limited

First published 2009

Copyright © 2009 Flame Tree Publishing

11 13 12 10
7 9 10 8 6

ISBN: 978-1-84786-455-0

All rights reserved. No part of this publication may be reproduced, stored in a retrieval system,
or transmitted in any form or by any means, electronic, mechanical, photocopying, recording or otherwise,
without the prior written permission of the publisher.

A copy of the CIP data for this book is available from the British Library.

Printed in China

Traditional Recipes

Quick and Easy, Proven Recipes

FLAME TREE
PUBLISHING

Contents

Contents

Meat 118

Poultry

Contents

Vegetables & Vegetarian   250

Puddings & Desserts

Nutrition
The Role of Essential Nutrients

A healthy and well-balanced diet is the body's primary energy source. In children, it constitutes the building blocks for future health as well as providing lots of energy. In adults, it encourages self-healing and regeneration within the body. A well-balanced diet will provide the body with all the essential nutrients it needs. This can be achieved by eating a variety of foods, demonstrated in the pyramid below:

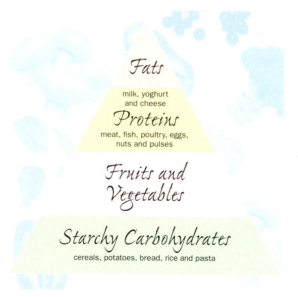

Fats

milk, yoghurt
and cheese

Proteins

meat, fish, poultry, eggs,
nuts and pulses

*Fruits and
Vegetables*

Starchy Carbohydrates

cereals, potatoes, bread, rice and pasta

Fats

Fats fall into two categories: saturated and unsaturated fats. It is very important that a healthy balance is achieved within the diet. Fats are an essential part of the diet and a source of energy and provide essential fatty acids and fat soluble vitamins. The right balance of fats should boost the body's immunity to infection and keep muscles, nerves and arteries in good condition. Saturated fats are of animal origin and are hard when stored at room temperature. They can be found in dairy produce, meat, eggs, margarines and hard white cooking fat (lard) as well as in manufactured products such as pies, biscuits and cakes. A high intake of saturated fat over many years has been proven to increase heart disease and high blood cholesterol levels and often leads to weight gain. The aim of a healthy diet is to keep the fat content low in the foods that we eat. Lowering the amount of saturated fat that we consume is very important, but this does not mean that it is good to consume lots of other types of fat.

There are two kinds of unsaturated fats: poly-unsaturated fats and monounsaturated fats. Poly-unsaturated fats include the following oils: safflower oil, soybean oil, corn oil and sesame oil. Within the poly-unsaturated group are Omega oils. The Omega-3 oils are of significant interest because they have been found to be particularly beneficial to coronary health and can encourage brain growth and development. Omega-3 oils are derived from oily fish such as salmon, mackerel, herring, pilchards and sardines. It is recommended that we should eat these types of fish at least once a week. However, for those who do not eat fish or who are vegetarians, liver oil supplements are available in most supermarkets and health shops. It is suggested that these supplements should be taken on a daily basis. The most popular oils that are high in monounsaturates are olive oil, sunflower oil and peanut oil. The Mediterranean diet, which is based on a diet high in mono-unsaturated fats, is recommended for heart health. Also, monounsaturated fats are known to help reduce the levels of LDL (the bad) cholestrol.

Proteins

Composed of amino acids (proteins' building bricks), proteins perform a wide variety of essential functions for the body including supplying energy and building and repairing tissues. Good sources of proteins are eggs, milk, yoghurt, cheese, meat, fish, poultry, eggs, nuts and pulses. (See the second level of the pyramid.) Some of these foods, however, contain saturated fats. To strike a nutritional balance eat generous amounts of vegetable protein foods such as soya, beans, lentils, peas and nuts.

Fruits and Vegetables

Not only are fruits and vegetables the most visually appealing foods, but they are extremely good for us, providing essential vitamins and minerals essential for growth, repair and protection in the human body. Fruits and vegetables are low in calories and are responsible for regulating the body's metabolic processes and controlling the composition of its fluids and cells.

Minerals

CALCIUM Important for healthy bones and teeth, nerve transmission, muscle contraction, blood clotting and hormone function. Calcium promotes a healthy heart, improves skin, relieves aching muscles and bones, maintains the correct acid-alkaline balance and reduces menstrual cramps. Good sources are dairy products, small bones of small fish, nuts, pulses, fortified white flours, breads and green leafy vegetables.

CHROMIUM Part of the glucose tolerance factor, chromium balances blood sugar levels, helps to normalise hunger and reduce cravings, improves lifespan, helps protect DNA and is essential for heart function. Good sources are brewer's yeast, wholemeal bread, rye bread, oysters, potatoes, green peppers, butter and parsnips.

IODINE Important for the manufacture of thyroid hormones and for normal development. Good sources of iodine are seafood, seaweed, milk and dairy products.

IRON As a component of haemoglobin, iron carries oxygen around the body. It is vital for normal growth and development. Good sources are liver, corned beef, red meat, fortified breakfast cereals, pulses, green leafy vegetables, egg yolk and cocoa and cocoa products.

MAGNESIUM Important for efficient functioning of metabolic enzymes and development of the skeleton. Magnesium promotes healthy muscles by helping them to relax and is therefore good for PMS. It is also important for heart muscles and the nervous system. Good sources are nuts, green vegetables, meat, cereals, milk and yoghurt.

PHOSPHORUS Forms and maintains bones and teeth, builds muscle tissue, helps maintain the body's pH and aids metabolism and energy production. Phosphorus is present in almost all foods.

POTASSIUM Enables nutrients to move into cells, while waste products move out; promotes healthy nerves and muscles; maintains fluid balance in the body; helps secretion of insulin for blood sugar control to produce constant energy; relaxes muscles; maintains heart functioning and stimulates gut movement to encourage proper elimination. Good sources are fruit, vegetables, milk and bread.

SELENIUM Antioxidant properties help to protect against free radicals and carcinogens. Selenium reduces inflammation, stimulates the immune system to fight infections, promotes a healthy heart and helps vitamin E's action. It is also required for the male reproductive system and is needed for metabolism. Good sources are tuna, liver, kidney, meat, eggs, cereals, nuts and dairy products.

SODIUM Important in helping to control body fluid and balance, preventing dehydration. Sodium is involved in muscle and nerve function and helps move nutrients into cells. All foods are good sources, however processed, pickled and salted foods are richest in sodium.

ZINC Important for metabolism and the healing of wounds. It also aids ability to cope with stress, promotes a healthy nervous system and brain especially in the growing foetus, aids bones and teeth formation and is essential for constant energy. Good sources are liver, meat, pulses, whole-grain cereals, nuts and oysters.

Vitamins

VITAMIN A Important for cell growth and development and for the formation of visual pigments in the eye. Vitamin A comes in two forms: retinol and beta-carotenes. Retinol is found in liver, meat and meat products and whole milk and its products. Beta-carotene is a powerful antioxidant and is found in red and yellow fruits and vegetables such as carrots, mangoes and apricots.

VITAMIN B1 Important in releasing energy from carboydrate-containing foods. Good sources are yeast and yeast products, bread, fortified breakfast cereals and potatoes.

VITAMIN B2 Important for metabolism of proteins, fats and carbohydrates to produce energy. Good sources are meat, yeast extracts, fortified breakfast cereals and milk and its products.

VITAMIN B3 Required for the metabolism of food into energy production. Good sources are milk and milk products, fortified breakfast cereals, pulses, meat, poultry and eggs.

VITAMIN B5 Important for the metabolism of food and energy production. All foods are good sources but especially fortified breakfast cereals, whole-grain bread and dairy products.

VITAMIN B6 Important for metabolism of protein and fat. Vitamin B6 may also be involved with the regulation of sex hormones. Good sources are liver, fish, pork, soya beans and peanuts.

VITAMIN B12 Important for the production of red blood cells and DNA. It is vital for growth and the nervous system. Good sources are meat, fish, eggs, poultry and milk.

BIOTIN Important for metabolism of fatty acids. Good sources of biotin are liver, kidney, eggs and nuts. Micro-organisms also manufacture this vitamin in the gut.

VITAMIN C Important for healing wounds and the formation of collagen which keeps skin and bones strong. It is an important antioxidant. Good sources are fruits, soft summer fruits and vegetables.

VITAMIN D Important for absorption and handling of calcium to help build bone strength. Good sources are oily fish, eggs, whole milk and milk products, margarine and of course sufficient exposure to sunlight, as vitamin D is made in the skin.

VITAMIN E Important as an antioxidant vitamin helping to protect cell membranes from damage. Good sources are vegetable oils, margarines, seeds, nuts and green vegetables.

FOLIC ACID Critical during pregnancy for the development of the brain and nerves. It is always essential for brain and nerve function and is needed for utilising protein and red blood cell formation. Good sources are whole-grain cereals, fortified breakfast cereals, green leafy vegetables, oranges and liver.

VITAMIN K Important for controlling blood clotting. Good sources are cauliflower, Brussels sprouts, lettuce, cabbage, beans, broccoli, peas, asparagus, potatoes, corn oil, tomatoes and milk.

Carbohydrates

Carbohydrates are an energy source and come in two forms: starch and sugar carbohydrates. Starch carbohydrates are also known as complex carbohydrates and they include all cereals, potatoes, breads, rice and pasta. (See the fourth level of the pyramid). Eating whole-grain varieties of these foods also provides fibre. Diets high in fibre are believed to be beneficial in helping to prevent bowel cancer and can also keep cholesterol down. High-fibre diets are also good for those concerned about weight gain. Fibre is bulky so fills the stomach, therefore reducing hunger pangs. Sugar carbohydrates, which are also known as fast-release carbohydrates (because of the quick fix of energy they give to the body), include sugar and sugar-sweetened products such as jams and syrups. Milk provides lactose, which is a milk sugar, and fruits provide fructose, which is a fruit sugar.

Cooking Techniques for Potatoes

Generally, new potato varieties have a firm and waxy texture that do not break up during cooking, so are ideal for boiling, steaming and salads. Main crop potatoes, on the other hand, have a more floury texture and lend themselves to mashing and roasting – both types are suitable for chips. When cooking potatoes, it is important to make sure the potatoes that you are using are the correct type for the dish being prepared. Whichever way you choose to serve potatoes, allow 175–225 g/6–8 oz per person.

Boiling Potatoes

NEW POTATOES Most of the new potatoes available nowadays are fairly clean – especially those sold in supermarkets – and simply need a light scrub before cooking in their skins. If the potatoes are very dirty, use a small scrubbing brush or scourer to remove both the skins and dirt. Add them to a pan of cold, salted water and bring to the boil. Cover the pan with a lid and simmer for 12–15 minutes or until tender. Add a couple of sprigs of fresh herbs to the pan if you like – fresh mint is traditionally used to flavour potatoes. Drain the potatoes thoroughly and serve hot, tossed in a little melted butter or for a change a tablespoon of pesto. The skins of first early new potatoes will peel away easily, but second earlies should be served in their skins or peeled when cooked (hold the hot potatoes with a fork to

make this easier). Very firm new potatoes can be added to boiling water, simmered for 8 minutes, and then left to stand in the hot water for a further 10 minutes until cooked through.

OLD POTATOES Choose a main crop potato suitable for boiling, then thinly peel and cut into even-sized pieces. Add to a saucepan of cold, salted water and bring to the boil. Cover the pan with a lid and simmer for 20 minutes or until tender.

Alternatively, you can cook the potatoes in their skins and peel them after cooking. (It is particularly important to cook floury potatoes gently or the outsides may start to fall apart before they are tender in the centre. Drain the potatoes in a colander, then return them to the pan to dry out over a very low heat for 1–2 minutes.) If you are planning to serve the potatoes mashed, roughly mash them and add a knob of butter and 2 tablespoons of milk per person. Mash until smooth, either with a hand masher, mouli grater or a potato ricer. Season to taste with salt, freshly ground black pepper and a little freshly grated nutmeg if liked, then beat for a few seconds with a wooden spoon until fluffy. As an alternative to butter, use a good-quality olive oil or crème fraîche. Finely chopped red and green chillies, crispy-cooked crumbled bacon, fresh herbs or grated Parmesan cheese can also be stirred in for additional flavour.

Steaming Potatoes

All potatoes are suitable for steaming. Floury potatoes, however, are ideal for this method of cooking as they fall apart easily. New and small potatoes can be steamed whole, but larger ones should be cut into even-sized pieces. Place the potatoes in a steamer, colander or sieve over boiling water and cover. Steam for 10 minutes if the potatoes are very small or if they are cut into large chunks cook for 20–25 minutes.

Frying Potatoes

CHIPPED POTATOES To make chipped potatoes (commonly known as chips), wash, peel and cut the potatoes into 1.5 cm/⅝ inch slices. Cut the slices into long strips about 1.5 cm/⅝ inches wide. Place the strips in a bowl of cold water and leave for 20 minutes, then drain and dry well on kitchen paper – moisture will make the fat spit. Pour some oil into a deep, heavy-based saucepan or deep-fat fryer, making sure that the oil does not go any further than halfway up the sides of the pan. Heat the oil to 190°C/375°F, or until a chip dropped into the fat rises to the surface straight away and is surrounded by bubbles. Put the chips into a wire basket and lower into the oil and cook for 7–8 minutes or until golden. Remove and increase the heat of the oil to 200°C/400°F. Lower the chips into the oil again and cook for 2–3 minutes, or until they are crisp and golden brown. Drain on kitchen paper before serving.

Slightly finer chips are known as 'pommes frites', even finer ones as 'pommes allumettes' and the finest of all as 'pommes pailles' (straw chips). Paper-thin slices of peeled potatoes, cut with a sharp knife or using a mandoline or food processor, can be deep-fried a few at a time to make crisps or game chips.

HEALTHY CHIPS To make lower-fat chips, preheat the oven to 200°C/400°F/Gas Mark 6 and place a non-stick baking tray in the oven to heat up. Cut the potatoes into chips as above or into chunky wedges, if preferred. Put the chips or wedges in a pan of cold water and quickly bring to the boil. Simmer for 2 minutes, then drain in a colander. Leave for a few minutes to dry, then drizzle over 1½–2 tablespoons of olive or sunflower oil and toss to coat. Tip on to the heated baking tray and cook in the preheated oven for 20–25 minutes, turning occasionally until golden brown and crisp.

SAUTÉED POTATOES

Cut peeled potatoes into rounds about 0.5 cm/¼ inch thick and pat dry. Heat 25 g/1 oz unsalted butter and 2 tablespoons of oil in a large, heavy-based frying pan until hot. Add the potatoes in a single layer and cook for 4–5 minutes until the undersides are golden. Turn with a large fish slice and cook the other side until golden and tender. Drain on kitchen paper and sprinkle with a little salt before serving.

Baking Potatoes

Allow a 300–350 g/11–12 oz potato per person and choose a variety such as Maris Piper, Cara or King Edward. Wash and dry the potatoes, prick the skins lightly, then rub each one with a little oil and sprinkle with salt. Bake at 200°C/400°F/ Gas Mark 6 for 1–1½ hours or until the skins are crisp and the centres are very soft. To speed up the cooking time, thread on to metal skewers as this conducts heat to the middle of the potatoes.

Roasting Potatoes

For crisp and brown outsides and fluffy centres choose potatoes suitable for baking. Thinly peel the potatoes and cut into even-sized pieces. Drop them into a pan of boiling, salted water and simmer for 5 minutes. Turn off the heat and leave for a further 3–4 minutes. Drain well and return the potatoes to the pan over a low heat for a minute to dry them and to roughen the edges. Carefully transfer them to a roasting tin containing hot oil or dripping. Baste well, then bake at 220°C/425°F/Gas Mark 7 for 20 minutes. Turn them and cook for a further 20–30 minutes, turning and basting at least one more time. Serve as soon as the potatoes are ready.

Potato Croquettes

Mash dry, boiled potatoes with just a little butter or olive oil, then stir in 1 egg yolk mixed with 1–2 tablespoons of milk or crème fraîche to make a firm mixture. Shape the mashed potatoes into small cylinders about 5 cm/2 inches long, rolling them in flour. Dip in beaten egg and then in fresh, white breadcrumbs. Chill the croquettes in the refrigerator for 30 minutes. Place a little unsalted butter and oil in a heavy-based frying pan and slowly heat until the butter has melted. Shallow fry the croquettes, turning occasionally until they are golden brown and crisp.

Rosti

Parboil peeled, waxy potatoes in boiling, salted water for 8 minutes, drain and leave to cool before coarsely grating into a bowl. Season well with salt and freshly ground black pepper and freshly chopped herbs if liked. Heat a mixture of unsalted butter and oil in a heavy-based frying pan until bubbling. Add tablespoonfuls of the grated potato into the pan and flatten with the back of a fish slice. Cook over a medium heat for about 7 minutes or until crisp and golden. Turn and cook the other side.

Cooking Potatoes in a Clay Pot

Terracotta potato pots can cook up to 450 g/1 lb of whole potatoes at a time. Soak the clay pot for at least 20 minutes before use, then add even-sized, preferably smallish potatoes. Drizzle over a little olive oil and season generously with salt and freshly ground black pepper. Cover the pot with the lid and put in a cold oven, setting the temperature to 200°C/400°F/Gas Mark 6. The potatoes will take about 45 minutes to cook.

Microwaved Potatoes

This method of cooking is suitable for boiling and baking potatoes, providing you do not want the skins to be crispy. To cook new potatoes, prick the skins with a skewer to prevent them from bursting, then place in a bowl with 3 tablespoons of boiling water. Cover with clingfilm which has been pierced two or three times and cook on High for 12–15 minutes, or until tender. Peeled chunks of potato can be cooked in the same way. To bake potatoes, place each potato on a circle of kitchen paper. Make several cuts in each to ensure that the skins do not burst. Transfer to the microwave plate and cook on High for 4–6 minutes per potato, allowing an extra 3–4 minutes for every additional potato. Turn the potatoes at least once during cooking. Leave to stand for 5 minutes before serving.

Health and Nutrition

Potatoes are high in complex carbohydrates, providing sustained energy. They are also an excellent source of vitamins B and C and minerals such as iron and potassium. They contain almost no fat and are high in dietary fibre.

Basic Baking Techniques

There is no mystery to successful baking, it really is easy providing you follow a few simple rules and guidelines. First, read the recipe right through before commencing. There is nothing more annoying than getting to the middle of a recipe and discovering that you are minus one or two of the ingredients. Until you are confident, follow a recipe, do not try a short cut otherwise you may find that you have left out a vital step which means that the recipe really cannot work. Most of all, have patience, baking is easy – if you can read, you can bake.

Pastry Making

Pastry needs to be kept as cool as possible through-out. Cool hands help, but are not essential. Use cold or iced water, but not too much as pastry does not need to be wet. Make sure that your fat is not runny or melted but firm (this is why block fat is the best). Avoid using too much flour when rolling out as this alters the proportions and also avoid handling the dough too much. Roll in one direction as this helps to ensure that

Hints for successful baking

Ensure that the ingredients are accurately measured. A cake that has too much flour or insufficient egg will be dry and crumbly. Take care when measuring the raising agent if used, as too much will mean that the cake will rise too quickly and then sink. Insufficient raising agent means the cake will not rise in the first place.

Ensure that the oven is preheated to the correct temperature, it can take 10 minutes to reach 180°C/350°F/Gas Mark 4. You may find that an oven thermometer is a good investment. Cakes are best if cooked in the centre of the preheated oven. Try to avoid opening the oven door at the start of cooking as a draft can make the cake sink. If using a fan oven refer to the manufacturers' instructions.

Check that the cake is thoroughly cooked by removing from the oven and inserting a clean skewer. Leave for 30 seconds and remove. If clean then the cake is cooked, if there is a little mixture return to the oven for a few minutes.

Other problems while cake making are insufficient creaming of the fat and sugar or a curdled creamed mixture (which will result in a fairly solid cake). Flour that has not been folded in carefully enough or has not been mixed with enough raising agent may also result in a fairly heavy consistency. Ensure that the correct size of tin is used as you may end up either with a flat, hard cake or one which has spilled over the edge of the tin. Be aware – especially when cooking with fruit – that if the consistency is too soft, the cake will not be able to support the fruit.

Finally, when you take your cake out of the oven, unless the recipe states that it should be left in the tin until cold, leave for a few minutes, then loosen the edges and turn out on to a wire rack to cool. Cakes which are left in the tin for too long, tend to sink or slightly overcook. When storing, make sure the cake is completely cold before placing it into an airtight tin or plastic container.

the pastry does not shrink. Allow the pastry to rest, preferably in the refrigerator after rolling. If you follow these guidelines but your pastry is still not as good as you would like it to be, then make it in a food processor instead.

Lining a Flan Case

It is important to choose the right tin to bake with. You will often find that a loose-bottomed metal flan case is the best option as it conducts heat more efficiently and evenly than a ceramic dish. It also has the advantage of a removable base which makes transferring the final flan easy; it simply lifts out keeping the pastry intact.

Roll the pastry out on a lightly floured surface ensuring that it is a few inches larger than the flan case. Wrap the pastry round the rolling pin, lift and place in the tin. Carefully ease the pastry into the base and sides of the tin, ensuring that there are no tears in the pastry. Allow to rest for a few minutes then trim the edge either with a sharp knife or by rolling a rolling pin across the top of the flan tin.

Baking Blind

The term baking blind means that the pastry case needs to be cooked without the filling, resulting in a crisp pastry shell that is either partially or fully cooked depending on whether the filling needs any cooking. Pastry shells can be prepared ahead of time as they last for several days if stored correctly in an airtight container or longer if frozen.

To bake blind, line a pastry case with the prepared pastry and allow to rest in the refrigerator for 30 minutes. This will help

to minimize shrinkage while it is being cooked. Remove from the refrigerator and lightly prick the base all over with a fork (do not do this if the filling is runny). Brush with a little beaten egg if desired or simply line the case with a large square of greaseproof paper, big enough to cover both the base and sides of the pastry case. Fill with either ceramic baking beans or dried beans. Place on a baking sheet and bake in a preheated oven, generally at 200°C/400°F/Gas Mark 6, remembering that ovens can take at least 15 minutes to reach this heat. Cook for 10–12 minutes, then remove from the oven, discard the paper and beans. Return to the oven and continue to cook for a further 5–10 minutes depending on whether the filling needs cooking. Normally, unless otherwise stated, individual pastry tartlet cases also benefit from baking blind.

Covering a Pie Dish

To cover a pie, roll out the pastry until it is about two inches larger than the circumference of the dish. Cut a 2.5 cm/ 1 inch strip from around the outside of the pastry and then moisten the edge of the pie dish you are using. Place the strip on the edge of the dish and brush with water or beaten egg. Generously fill the pie dish until the surface is slightly rounded. Using the rolling pin, lift the remaining pastry and cover the pie dish. Press together, then seal. Using a sharp knife, trim off any excess pastry from around the edges. Try to avoid brushing the edges of the pastry especially puff pastry as this prevents the pastry rising evenly. Before placing in the oven make a small hole in the centre of the pie to allow the steam to escape.

The edges of the pie can be forked by pressing the back of a fork around the edge of the pie or instead crimp by pinching the edge crust holding the thumb and index finger of your right hand against the edge while gently pushing with the index finger of your left hand. Other ways of finishing the pie are to knock up (achieved by gently pressing your index finger down

on to the rim and, at the same time, tapping a knife horizontally along the edge giving it a flaky appearance), or fluting the edges by pressing your thumb down on the edge of the pastry while gently drawing back an all-purpose knife about 1 cm/½ inch and repeating around the rim. Experiment by putting leaves and berries made out of leftover pastry to finish off the pie, then brush the top of the pie with beaten egg.

Lining Cake Tins

If a recipe states that the tin needs lining do not be tempted to ignore this. Rich fruit cakes and other cakes that take a long time to cook benefit from the tin being lined so that the edges and base do not burn or dry out. Greaseproof or baking parchment paper is ideal for this. It is a good idea to have the paper at least double thickness, or preferably 3–4 thicknesses. Sponge cakes and other cakes that are cooked in 30 minutes or less are also better if the bases are lined as it is far easier to remove them from the tin.

The best way to line a round or square tin is to lightly draw around the base and then cut just inside the markings making it easy to sit in the tin. Next, lightly oil the paper so it easily peels away from the cake. If the sides of the tin also need to be lined, then cut a strip of paper long enough for the tin. This can be measured by wrapping a piece of string around the rim of the tin. Once again, lightly oil the paper, push against the tin and oil once more as this will hold the paper to the sides of the tin. Steamed puddings usually need only a disc of greaseproof paper at the bottom of the dish as the sides come away easily.

Soups
& Starters

Tomato & Basil Soup

SERVES 4

1.1 kg/ 2½ lb ripe
   tomatoes, cut in half
2 garlic cloves
1 tsp olive oil
1 tbsp balsamic vinegar

1 tbsp dark brown sugar
1 tbsp tomato purée
300 ml/½ pint
   vegetable stock
6 tbsp natural yogurt

2 tbsp freshly chopped basil
salt and freshly ground
   black pepper
small basil leaves,
   to garnish

Preheat the oven to 200°C/400°F/Gas Mark 6. Evenly spread the tomatoes and unpeeled garlic in a single layer in a large roasting tin. Mix the oil and vinegar together. Drizzle over the tomatoes and sprinkle with the dark brown sugar. Roast the tomatoes in the preheated oven for 20 minutes until tender and lightly charred in places.

Remove from the oven and allow to cool slightly. When cool enough to handle, squeeze the softened flesh of the garlic from the papery skin. Place with the charred tomatoes in a nylon sieve over a saucepan.

Press the garlic and tomato through the sieve with the back of a wooden spoon. When all the flesh has been sieved, add the tomato purée and vegetable stock to the pan. Heat gently, stirring occasionally.

In a small bowl, beat the yogurt and basil together and season to taste with salt and pepper. Stir the basil yogurt into the soup. Garnish with basil leaves and serve immediately.

Try this: FOR AN ALTERNATIVE: 28 FOR A MAIN COURSE: 80

Rice & Tomato Soup

SERVES 4

150 g/5 oz easy-cook
  basmati rice
400 g can chopped tomatoes
2 garlic cloves, peeled
  and crushed
grated rind of ½ lime
2 tbsp extra virgin olive oil

1 tsp sugar
salt and freshly
  ground pepper
300 ml/½ pint vegetable
  stock or water

For the croûtons:
2 tbsp prepared pesto sauce
2 tbsp olive oil
6 thin slices ciabatta
  bread, cut into
  1 cm/½ inch cubes

Preheat the oven to 220°C/425°F/Gas Mark 7. Rinse and drain the basmati rice. Place the canned tomatoes with their juice in a large, heavy-based saucepan with the garlic, lime rind, oil and sugar. Season to taste with salt and pepper. Bring to the boil, then reduce the heat, cover and simmer for 10 minutes.

Add the boiling vegetable stock or water and the rice, then cook, uncovered, for a further 15–20 minutes, or until the rice is tender. If the soup is too thick, add a little more water. Reserve and keep warm, if the croûtons are not ready.

Meanwhile, to make the croûtons, mix the pesto and olive oil in a large bowl. Add the bread cubes and toss until they are coated completely with the mixture. Spread on a baking sheet and bake in the preheated oven for 10–15 minutes, until golden and crisp, turning them over halfway through cooking. Serve the soup immediately sprinkled with the warm croûtons.

Try this: FOR AN ALTERNATIVE: 24   FOR A MAIN COURSE: 176

Roasted Red Pepper, Tomato & Red Onion Soup

SERVES 4

fine spray of oil
2 large red peppers,
    deseeded and
    roughly chopped
1 red onion, peeled and
    roughly chopped

350 g/12 oz
    tomatoes, halved
1 small crusty French loaf
1 garlic clove, peeled
600 ml/1 pint
    vegetable stock

salt and freshly ground
    black pepper
1 tsp Worcestershire sauce
4 tbsp fromage frais

Preheat the oven to 190°C/375°F/Gas Mark 5. Spray a large roasting tin with the oil and place the peppers and onion in the base. Cook in the oven for 10 minutes. Add the tomatoes and cook for a further 20 minutes or until the peppers are soft.

Cut the bread into 1 cm/½ inch slices. Cut the garlic clove in half and rub the cut edge of the garlic over the bread. Place all the bread slices on a large baking tray, and bake in the preheated oven for 10 minutes, turning halfway through, until golden and crisp.

Remove the vegetables from the oven and allow to cool slightly, then blend in a food processor until smooth. Strain the vegetable mixture through a large nylon sieve into a saucepan, to remove the seeds and skin. Add the stock, season to taste with salt and pepper and stir to mix. Heat the soup gently until piping hot.

In a small bowl beat together the Worcestershire sauce with the fromage frais. Pour the soup into warmed bowls and swirl a spoonful of the fromage frais mixture into each bowl. Serve immediately with the garlic toasts.

Try this: FOR AN ALTERNATIVE: 26   FOR A MAIN COURSE: 156

Curried Parsnip Soup

SERVES 4

1 tsp cumin seeds
2 tsp coriander seeds
1 tsp oil
1 onion, peeled
   and chopped
1 garlic clove, peeled
   and crushed

½ tsp turmeric
¼ tsp chilli powder
1 cinnamon stick
450 g/1 lb parsnips, peeled
   and chopped
1 litre/1¾ pint
   vegetable stock

salt and freshly ground
   black pepper
2–3 tbsp natural yogurt,
   to serve
fresh coriander leaves,
   to garnish

In a small frying pan, dry-fry the cumin and coriander seeds over a moderately high heat for 1–2 minutes. Shake the pan during cooking until the seeds are lightly toasted. Reserve until cooled. Grind the toasted seeds in a pestle and mortar.

Heat the oil in a saucepan. Cook the onion until softened and starting to turn golden. Add the garlic, turmeric, chilli powder and cinnamon stick to the pan. Continue to cook for a further minute.

Add the parsnips and stir well. Pour in the stock and bring to the boil. Cover and simmer for 15 minutes or until the parsnips are cooked.

Allow the soup to cool. Once cooled, remove the cinnamon stick and discard. Blend the soup in a food processor until very smooth.

Transfer to a saucepan and reheat gently. Season to taste with salt and pepper. Garnish with fresh coriander and serve immediately with the yogurt.

Try this: FOR AN ALTERNATIVE: 32   FOR A MAIN COURSE: 286

Swede, Turnip, Parsnip & Potato Soup

SERVES 4

2 large onions, peeled
25 g/1 oz butter
2 medium carrots, peeled
  and roughly chopped
175 g/6 oz swede, peeled
  and roughly chopped
125 g/4 oz turnip, peeled and

roughly chopped
125 g/4 oz parsnips, peeled
  and roughly chopped
175 g/6 oz potatoes, peeled
1 litre/1¾ pints
  vegetable stock
½ tsp freshly

grated nutmeg
salt and freshly ground
  black pepper
4 tbsp vegetable oil,
  for frying
125 ml/4 fl oz double cream
warm crusty bread, to serve

Finely chop 1 onion. Melt the butter in a large saucepan and add the onion, carrots, swede, turnip, parsnip and potatoes. Cover and cook gently for about 10 minutes, without colouring. Stir occasionally during this time.

Add the stock and season to taste with the nutmeg, salt and pepper. Cover and bring to the boil, then reduce the heat and simmer gently for 15–20 minutes, or until the vegetables are tender. Remove from the heat and leave to cool for 30 minutes.

Heat the oil in a large, heavy-based frying pan. Add the onions and cook over a medium heat for about 2–3 minutes, stirring frequently, until golden brown. Remove the onions with a slotted spoon and drain well on absorbent kitchen paper. As they cool, they will turn crispy.

Pour the cooled soup into a food processor or blender and process to form a smooth purée. Return to the cleaned pan, adjust the seasoning, then stir in the cream. Gently reheat and top with the crispy onions. Serve immediately with chunks of bread.

Try this: FOR AN ALTERNATIVE: 30 FOR A MAIN COURSE: 152

Potato, Leek & Rosemary Soup

SERVES 4

50 g/2 oz butter
450 g/1 lb leeks, trimmed
   and finely sliced
700 g/1½ lb potatoes,
   peeled and
   roughly chopped

900 ml/1½ pints
   vegetable stock
4 sprigs of fresh rosemary
450 ml/¾ pint
   full-cream milk
2 tbsp freshly

chopped parsley
2 tbsp crème fraîche
salt and freshly ground
   black pepper
wholemeal rolls,
   to serve

Melt the butter in a large saucepan, add the leeks and cook gently for 5 minutes, stirring frequently. Remove 1 tablespoon of the cooked leeks and reserve for garnishing.

Add the potatoes, vegetable stock, rosemary sprigs and milk. Bring to the boil, then reduce the heat, cover and simmer gently for 20–25 minutes, or until the vegetables are tender.

Cool for 10 minutes. Discard the rosemary, then pour into a food processor or blender and blend well to form a smooth-textured soup.

Return the soup to the cleaned saucepan and stir in the chopped parsley and crème fraîche. Season to taste with salt and pepper. If the soup is too thick, stir in a little more milk or water. Reheat gently without boiling, then ladle into warm soup bowls. Garnish the soup with the reserved leeks and serve immediately with wholemeal rolls.

Try this: FOR AN ALTERNATIVE: 32   FOR A MAIN COURSE: 208

Carrot & Ginger Soup

SERVES 4

4 slices of bread,
  crusts removed
1 tsp yeast extract
2 tsp olive oil
1 onion, peeled
  and chopped
1 garlic clove, peeled
  and crushed

½ tsp ground ginger
450 g/1 lb carrots, peeled
  and chopped
1 litre/1¾ pint
  vegetable stock
2.5 cm/1 inch piece of
  root ginger, peeled and
  finely grated

salt and freshly ground
  black pepper
1 tbsp lemon juice

To garnish:
chives
lemon zest

Preheat the oven to 180°C/350°F/Gas Mark 4. Roughly chop the bread. Dissolve the yeast extract in 2 tablespoons of warm water and mix with the bread.

Spread the bread cubes over a lightly oiled baking tray and bake for 20 minutes, turning half way through. Remove from the oven and reserve.

Heat the oil in a large saucepan. Gently cook the onion and garlic for 3–4 minutes. Stir in the ground ginger and cook for 1 minute to release the flavour. Add the chopped carrots, then stir in the stock and the fresh ginger. Simmer gently for 15 minutes.

Remove from the heat and allow to cool a little. Blend until smooth, then season to taste with salt and pepper. Stir in the lemon juice. Garnish with the chives and lemon zest and serve immediately.

 Try this: FOR AN ALTERNATIVE: 26   FOR A MAIN COURSE: 126

Cream of Spinach Soup

SERVES 6-8

1 large onion, peeled
    and chopped
5 large plump garlic cloves,
    peeled and chopped
2 medium potatoes, peeled
    and chopped
750 ml/1¼ pints cold water

1 tsp salt
450 g/1 lb spinach, washed
    and large stems removed
50 g/2 oz butter
3 tbsp flour
750 ml/1¼ pints milk
½ tsp freshly

grated nutmeg
freshly ground black pepper
6–8 tbsp crème fraîche or
    soured cream
warm foccacia bread,
    to serve

Place the onion, garlic and potatoes in a large saucepan and cover with the cold water. Add half the salt and bring to the boil. Cover and simmer for 15–20 minutes, or until the potatoes are tender. Remove from the heat and add the spinach. Cover and set aside for 10 minutes.

Slowly melt the butter in another saucepan, add the flour and cook over a low heat for about 2 minutes. Remove the saucepan from the heat and add the milk, a little at a time, stirring continuously. Return to the heat and cook, stirring continuously, for 5–8 minutes, or until the sauce is smooth and slightly thickened. Add the freshly grated nutmeg, or to taste.

Blend the cooled potato and spinach mixture in a food processor or blender to a smooth purée, then return to the saucepan and gradually stir in the white sauce. Season to taste with salt and pepper and gently reheat, taking care not to allow the soup to boil. Ladle into soup bowls and top with spoonfuls of crème fraîche or soured cream. Serve immediately with warm foccacia bread.

Try this: FOR AN ALTERNATIVE: 30   FOR A MAIN COURSE: 180

Classic Minestrone

SERVES 6–8

25 g/1 oz butter
3 tbsp olive oil
3 rashers streaky bacon
1 large onion, peeled
1 garlic clove, peeled
1 celery stick, trimmed
2 carrots, peeled

400 g can chopped tomatoes
1.1 litre/2 pints chicken stock
175 g/6 oz green cabbage,
    finely shredded
50 g/2 oz French beans,
    trimmed and halved
3 tbsp frozen petits pois

50 g/2 oz spaghetti, broken
    into short pieces
salt and freshly ground
    black pepper
Parmesan cheese shavings,
    to garnish
crusty bread, to serve

Heat the butter and olive oil together in a large saucepan. Chop the bacon and add to the saucepan. Cook for 3–4 minutes, then remove with a slotted spoon and reserve.

Finely chop the onion, garlic, celery and carrots and add to the saucepan, one ingredient at a time, stirring well after each addition. Cover and cook gently for 8–10 minutes, until the vegetables are softened.

Add the chopped tomatoes, with their juice and the stock, bring to the boil then cover the saucepan with a lid, reduce the heat and simmer gently for about 20 minutes.

Stir in the cabbage, beans, peas and spaghetti pieces. Cover and simmer for a further 20 minutes, or until all the ingredients are tender. Season to taste with salt and pepper.

Return the cooked bacon to the saucepan and bring the soup to the boil. Serve the soup immediately with Parmesan cheese shavings sprinkled on the top and plenty of crusty bread to accompany it.

Try this: FOR AN ALTERNATIVE: 42   FOR A MAIN COURSE: 220

Bacon & Split Pea Soup

SERVES 4

50 g/2 oz dried split peas
25 g/1 oz butter
1 garlic clove, peeled and finely chopped
1 medium onion, peeled and thinly sliced
175 g/6 oz long-grain rice

2 tbsp tomato purée
1.1 litres/2 pints vegetable or chicken stock
175 g/6 oz carrots, peeled and finely diced
125 g/4 oz streaky bacon, finely chopped

salt and freshly ground black pepper
2 tbsp freshly chopped parsley
4 tbsp single cream
warm crusty garlic bread, to serve

Cover the dried split peas with plenty of cold water, cover loosely and leave to soak for a minimum of 12 hours, preferably overnight.

Melt the butter in a heavy-based saucepan, add the garlic and onion and cook for 2–3 minutes, without colouring. Add the rice, drained split peas and tomato purée and cook for 2–3 minutes, stirring constantly to prevent sticking. Add the stock, bring to the boil, then reduce the heat and simmer for 20–25 minutes, or until the rice and peas are tender. Remove from the heat and leave to cool.

Blend about three quarters of the soup in a food processor or blender to form a smooth purée. Pour the purée into the remaining soup in the saucepan. Add the carrots to the saucepan and cook for a further 10–12 minutes, or until the carrots are tender.

Meanwhile, place the bacon in a non-stick frying pan and cook over a gentle heat until the bacon is crisp. Remove and drain on absorbent kitchen paper.

Season the soup with salt and pepper to taste, then stir in the parsley and cream. Reheat for 2–3 minutes, then ladle into soup bowls. Sprinkle with the bacon and serve immediately with warm garlic bread.

Try this: FOR AN ALTERNATIVE: 26   FOR A MAIN COURSE: 136

Cawl

SERVES 4

700 g/1½ lb scrag end
  of lamb or best end of
  neck chops
pinch of salt
2 large onions, peeled and
  thinly sliced
3 large potatoes, peeled and

cut into chunks
2 parsnips, peeled and cut
  into chunks
1 swede, peeled and cut
  into chunks
3 large carrots, peeled and
  cut into chunks

2 leeks, trimmed and sliced
freshly ground black pepper
4 tbsp freshly chopped
  parsley
warm crusty bread, to serve

Put the lamb in a large saucepan, cover with cold water and bring to the boil. Add a generous pinch of salt. Simmer gently for 1½ hours, then set aside to cool completely, preferably overnight.

The next day, skim the fat off the surface of the lamb liquid and discard. Return the saucepan to the heat and bring back to the boil. Simmer for 5 minutes. Add the onions, potatoes, parsnips, swede and carrots and return to the boil. Reduce the heat, cover and cook for about 20 minutes, stirring occasionally.

Add the leeks and season to taste with salt and pepper. Cook for a further 10 minutes, or until all the vegetables are tender.

Using a slotted spoon, remove the meat from the saucepan and take the meat off the bone. Discard the bones and any gristle, then return the meat to the pan. Adjust the seasoning to taste, stir in the parsley, then serve immediately with plenty of warm crusty bread.

Try this: FOR AN ALTERNATIVE: 40   FOR A MAIN COURSE: 104

Cullen Skink

SERVES 4

25 g/1 oz unsalted butter
1 onion, peeled and
 chopped
1 fresh bay leaf
25 g/1 oz plain flour
350 g/12 oz new potatoes,
 scrubbed and cut into
 small pieces

600 ml/1 pint semi-skimmed
 milk
300 ml/½ pint water
350 g/12 oz undyed smoked
 haddock fillet, skinned
75 g/3 oz sweetcorn kernels
50 g/2 oz garden peas
freshly ground black pepper

½ tsp freshly grated nutmeg
2–3 tbsp single cream
2 tbsp freshly chopped
 parsley
crusty bread, to serve

Melt the butter in a large, heavy-based saucepan, add the onion and cook for 3 minutes, stirring occasionally. Add the bay leaf and stir, then sprinkle in the flour and cook over a low heat for 2 minutes, stirring frequently. Add the potatoes.

Take off the heat and gradually stir in the milk and water. Return to the heat and bring to the boil, stirring. Reduce the heat to a simmer and cook for 10 minutes.

Meanwhile, discard any pin bones from the fish and cut into small pieces. Add to the pan together with the sweetcorn and peas. Cover and cook gently, stirring occasionally, for 10 minutes, or until the vegetables and fish are cooked.

Add pepper and nutmeg to taste, then stir in the cream and heat gently for 1–2 minutes, or until piping hot Sprinkle with the parsley and serve with crusty bread.

Try this: FOR AN ALTERNATIVE: 50   FOR A MAIN COURSE: 204

Bouillabaisse

SERVES 4

675 g/1½ lb assorted fish,
   such as whiting, mackerel,
   red mullet, salmon and
   king prawns, cleaned
   and skinned
few saffron strands
3 tbsp olive oil

2 onions, peeled and sliced
2 celery sticks, trimmed and
   sliced
225 g/8 oz ripe tomatoes,
   peeled and chopped
1 fresh bay leaf
2–3 garlic cloves,

   peeled and crushed
1 bouquet garni
sea salt and freshly ground
black pepper
French bread, to serve

Cut the fish into thick pieces, peel the prawns, if necessary, and rinse well. Place the saffron strands in a small bowl, cover with warm water and leave to infuse for at least 10 minutes.

Heat the oil in a large, heavy-based saucepan or casserole, add the onions and celery and sauté for 5 minutes, stirring occasionally. Add the tomatoes, bay leaf, garlic and bouquet garni and stir until lightly coated with the oil.

Place the firm fish on top of the tomatoes and pour in the saffron-infused water and enough water to just cover. Bring to the boil, reduce the heat, cover with a lid and cook for 8 minutes.

Add the soft-flesh fish and continue to simmer for 5 minutes, or until all the fish are cooked. Season to taste with salt and pepper, remove and discard the bouquet garni and serve with French bread.

Try this: FOR AN ALTERNATIVE: 52   FOR A MAIN COURSE: 180

Pumpkin & Smoked Haddock Soup

SERVES 4

2 tbsp olive oil
1 medium onion, peeled and chopped
2 garlic cloves, peeled and chopped
3 celery stalks, trimmed and chopped

700 g/1½ lb pumpkin, peeled, deseeded and cut into chunks
450 g/1 lb potatoes, peeled and cut into chunks
750 ml/1¼ pints chicken stock, heated

125 ml/4 fl oz dry sherry
200 g/7 oz smoked haddock fillet
150 ml/¼ pint milk
freshly ground black pepper
2 tbsp freshly chopped parsley

Heat the oil in a large heavy-based saucepan and gently cook the onion, garlic, and celery for about 10 minutes. This will release the sweetness but not colour the vegetables. Add the pumpkin and potatoes to the saucepan and stir to coat the vegetables with the oil.

Gradually pour in the stock and bring to the boil. Cover, then reduce the heat and simmer for 25 minutes, stirring occasionally. Stir in the dry sherry, then remove the saucepan from the heat and leave to cool for 5–10 minutes. Blend the mixture in a food processor or blender to form a chunky purée and return to the cleaned saucepan.

Meanwhile, place the fish in a shallow frying pan. Pour in the milk with 3 tablespoons of water and bring to almost boiling point. Reduce the heat, cover and simmer for 6 minutes, or until the fish is cooked and flakes easily. Remove from the heat and, using a slotted spoon remove the fish from the liquid, reserving both liquid and fish.

Discard the skin and any bones from the fish and flake into pieces. Stir the fish liquid into the soup, together with the flaked fish. Season with freshly ground black pepper, stir in the parsley and serve immediately.

Try this: FOR AN ALTERNATIVE: 46   FOR A MAIN COURSE: 280

Sweetcorn & Crab Soup

SERVES 4

450 g/1 lb fresh
corn-on-the-cob
1.3 litres/2¼ pints
chicken stock
2–3 spring onions, trimmed
and finely chopped
1 cm/½ inch piece fresh root
ginger, peeled and

finely chopped
1 tbsp dry sherry or Chinese
rice wine
2–3 tsp soy sauce
1 tsp soft light brown sugar
salt and freshly ground
black pepper
2 tsp cornflour

225 g/8 oz white crabmeat,
fresh or canned
1 medium egg white
1 tsp sesame oil
1–2 tbsp freshly
chopped coriander

Wash the corns cobs and dry. Using a sharp knife and holding the corn cobs at an angle to the cutting board, cut down along the cobs to remove the kernels, then scrape the cobs to remove any excess milky residue. Put the kernels and the milky residue into a large wok.

Add the chicken stock to the wok and place over a high heat. Bring to the boil, stirring and pressing some of the kernels against the side of the wok to squeeze out the starch to help thicken the soup. Simmer for 15 minutes, stirring occasionally.

Add the spring onions, ginger, sherry or Chinese rice wine, soy sauce and brown sugar to the wok and season to taste with salt and pepper. Simmer for a further 5 minutes, stirring occasionally. Blend the cornflour with 1 tablespoon of cold water to form a smooth paste and whisk into the soup. Return to the boil, then simmer over medium heat until thickened.

Add the crabmeat, stirring until blended. Beat the egg white with the sesame oil and stir into the soup in a slow steady stream, stirring constantly. Stir in the chopped coriander and serve immediately.

Try this: FOR AN ALTERNATIVE: 54 FOR A MAIN COURSE: 192

Tuna Chowder

SERVES 4

2 tsp oil
1 onion, peeled and
  finely chopped
2 sticks of celery, trimmed
  and finely sliced
1 tbsp plain flour

600 ml/1 pint milk
200 g can tuna in water
320 g can sweetcorn in
  water, drained
2 tsp freshly chopped thyme
salt and freshly ground

black pepper
pinch cayenne pepper
2 tbsp freshly
  chopped parsley

Heat the oil in a large, heavy-based saucepan. Add the onion and celery and gently cook for about 5 minutes, stirring from time to time until the onion is softened.

Stir in the flour and cook for about 1 minute to thicken. Draw the pan off the heat and gradually pour in the milk, stirring throughout.

Add the tuna and its liquid, the drained sweetcorn and the thyme. Mix gently, then bring to the boil. Cover and simmer for 5 minutes. Remove the pan from the heat and season to taste with salt and pepper.

Sprinkle the chowder with the cayenne pepper and chopped parsley. Divide into soup bowls and serve immediately.

Try this: FOR AN ALTERNATIVE: 52 FOR A MAIN COURSE: 154

Creamy Salmon
with Dill in Filo Baskets

SERVES 4

1 bay leaf
6 black peppercorns
1 large sprig fresh parsley
175 g/6 oz salmon fillet
4 large sheets filo pastry

fine spray of oil
125 g/4 oz baby
    spinach leaves
8 tbsp fromage frais
2 tsp Dijon mustard

2 tbsp freshly chopped dill
salt and freshly ground
    black pepper

Preheat the oven to 200°C/400°F/Gas Mark 6. Place the bay leaf, peppercorns, parsley and salmon in a frying pan and add enough water to barely cover the fish.

Bring to the boil, reduce the heat and poach the fish for 5 minutes until it flakes easily. Remove it from the pan. Reserve.

Spray each sheet of filo pastry lightly with the oil. Scrunch up the pastry to make a nest shape approximately 12.5 cm/5 inches in diameter.

Place on a lightly oiled baking sheet and cook in the preheated oven for 10 minutes until golden and crisp.

Blanch the spinach in a pan of lightly salted boiling water for 2 minutes. Drain thoroughly and keep warm.

Mix the fromage frais, mustard and dill together, then warm gently. Season to taste with salt and pepper. Divide the spinach between the filo pastry nests and flake the salmon on to the spinach.

Spoon the mustard and dill sauce over the filo baskets and serve immediately.

Try this: FOR AN ALTERNATIVE: 58 FOR A MAIN COURSE: 130

Potato Pancakes with Smoked Salmon

SERVES 4

450 g/1 lb floury potatoes, peeled and quartered
salt and freshly ground black pepper
1 large egg
1 large egg yolk
25 g/1 oz butter

25 g/1 oz plain flour
150 ml/¼ pint double cream
2 tbsp freshly chopped parsley
5 tbsp crème fraîche
1 tbsp horseradish sauce
225 g/8 oz smoked

salmon, sliced
salad leaves, to serve

To garnish:
lemon slices
snipped chives

Cook the potatoes in a saucepan of lightly salted boiling water for 15–20 minutes, or until tender. Drain thoroughly, then mash until free of lumps. Beat in the whole egg and egg yolk, together with the butter. Beat until smooth and creamy. Slowly beat in the flour and cream, then season to taste with salt and pepper. Stir in the chopped parsley.

Beat the crème fraîche and horseradish sauce together in a small bowl, cover with cling-film and reserve.

Heat a lightly oiled, heavy-based frying pan over a medium-high heat. Place a few spoonfuls of the potato mixture in the hot pan and cook for 4–5 minutes, or until cooked and golden, turning halfway through cooking time. Remove from the pan, drain on absorbent kitchen paper and keep warm. Repeat with the remaining mixture.

Arrange the pancakes on individual serving plates. Place the smoked salmon on the pancakes and spoon over a little of the horseradish sauce. Serve with salad and the remaining horseradish sauce and garnish with lemon slices and chives.

Try this: FOR AN ALTERNATIVE: 56   FOR A MAIN COURSE: 166

Smoked Mackerel Vol-au-Vents

SERVES 1-2

350 g/12 oz prepared
  puff pastry
1 small egg, beaten
2 tsp sesame seeds
225 g/8 oz peppered smoked

mackerel, skinned
  and chopped
5 cm/2 inch piece cucumber
4 tbsp soft cream cheese
2 tbsp cranberry sauce

1 tbsp freshly chopped dill
1 tbsp finely grated
  lemon rind
dill sprigs, to garnish
mixed salad leaves, to serve

Preheat the oven to 230°C/450°F/Gas Mark 8. Roll the pastry out on a lightly floured surface and using a 9 cm/3½ inch fluted cutter, cut out 12 rounds. Using a 1 cm/½ inch cutter mark a lid in the centre of each round. Place on a damp baking sheet and brush the rounds with a little beaten egg.

Sprinkle the pastry with the sesame seeds and bake in the preheated oven for 10–12 minutes, or until golden brown and well risen. Transfer the vol-au-vents to a chopping board and when cool enough to touch carefully remove the lids with a small sharp knife.

Scoop out any uncooked pastry from the inside of each vol-au-vent, then return to the oven for 5–8 minutes to dry out. Remove and allow to cool.

Flake the mackerel into small pieces and reserve. Peel the cucumber if desired, cut into very small dice and add to the mackerel.

Beat the soft cream cheese with the cranberry sauce, dill and lemon rind. Stir in the mackerel and cucumber and use to fill the vol-au-vents. Place the lids on top and garnish dill sprigs.

Try this: FOR AN ALTERNATIVE: 50 FOR A MAIN COURSE: 140

Sesame Prawn Toasts

SERVES 4

125 g/4 oz peeled
  cooked prawns
1 tbsp cornflour
2 spring onions, peeled and
  roughly chopped
2 tsp freshly grated

root ginger
2 tsp dark soy sauce
pinch of Chinese five spice
  powder (optional)
1 small egg, beaten
salt and freshly ground

black pepper
6 thin slices day-old
  white bread
40 g/1½ oz sesame seeds
vegetable oil for deep-frying
chilli sauce, to serve

Place the prawns in a food processor or blender with the cornflour, spring onions, ginger, soy sauce and Chinese five spice powder, if using. Blend to a fairly smooth paste. Spoon into a bowl and stir in the beaten egg. Season to taste with salt and pepper.

Cut the crusts off the bread. Spread the prawn paste in an even layer on one side of each slice. Sprinkle over the sesame seeds and press down lightly.

Cut each slice diagonally into four triangles. Place on a board and chill in the refrigerator for 30 minutes.

Pour sufficient oil into a heavy-based saucepan or deep-fat fryer so that it is one third full. Heat until it reaches a temperature of 180°C/350°F. Cook the toasts in batches of five or six, carefully lowering them seeded-side down into the oil. Deep-fry for 2–3 minutes, or until lightly browned, then turn over and cook for 1 minute more. Using a slotted spoon, lift out the toasts and drain on absorbent kitchen paper. Keep warm while frying the remaining toasts. Arrange on a warmed platter and serve immediately with some chilli sauce for dipping.

Try this: FOR AN ALTERNATIVE: 52 FOR A MAIN COURSE: 164

Spring Rolls

MAKES 26–30 ROLLS

For the filling:
15 g/½ oz dried Chinese
  (shiitake) mushrooms
50 g/2 oz rice vermicelli
1–2 tbsp groundnut oil
1 small onion, peeled and
  finely chopped
3–4 garlic cloves, peeled and
  finely chopped
4 cm/1½ inch piece fresh
  root ginger, peeled

and chopped
225 g/8 oz fresh pork mince
2 spring onions, trimmed
  and finely chopped
75 g/3 oz beansprouts
4 water chestnuts, chopped
2 tbsp freshly
  snipped chives
175 g/6 oz cooked peeled
  prawns, chopped
1 tsp oyster sauce

1 tsp soy sauce
salt and freshly ground
  black pepper
spring onion tassels,
  to garnish

For the wrappers:
4–5 tbsp plain flour
26–30 spring roll wrappers
300 ml/½ pint vegetable oil
  for deep frying

Soak the Chinese mushrooms in almost boiling water for 20 minutes. Remove and squeeze out the liquid. Discard any stems, slice and reserve. Soak the rice vermicelli as per the packet instructions. Heat a large wok and when hot, add the oil. Heat then add the onion, garlic and ginger and stir-fry for 2 minutes. Add the pork, spring onions and Chinese mushrooms and stir-fry for 4 minutes. Stir in the beansprouts, water chestnuts, chives, prawns, oyster and soy sauce. Season to taste with salt and pepper and spoon into a bowl. Drain the noodles well, add to the bowl and toss until well mixed, then leave to cool.

Blend the flour to a smooth paste with 3–4 tablespoons of water. Soften a wrapper in a plate of warm water for 1–2 seconds, then drain. Put 2 tablespoons of the filling near one edge of the wrapper, fold the edge over the filling, then fold in each side and roll up. Seal with a little flour paste and transfer to a baking sheet, seam-side down. Repeat with the remaining wrappers. Heat the oil in a large wok to 190°C/375°F, or until a cube of bread browns in 30 seconds. Fry the spring rolls a few at a time, until golden. Remove and drain on absorbent kitchen paper. Arrange on a serving plate and garnish with spring onion tassels. Serve immediately.

Sweet & Sour Spareribs

SERVES 4

1.6 kg/3½ lb pork spareribs
4 tbsp clear honey
1 tbsp Worcestershire sauce
1 tsp Chinese five
   spice powder

4 tbsp soy sauce
2½ tbsp dry sherry
1 tsp chilli sauce
2 garlic cloves, peeled
   and chopped

1½ tbsp tomato purée
1 tsp dry mustard
   powder (optional)
spring onion curls,
   to garnish

Preheat the oven to 200°C/400°F/Gas Mark 6, 15 minutes before cooking. If necessary, place the ribs on a chopping board and using a sharp knife, cut the joint in between the ribs, to form single ribs. Place the ribs in a shallow dish in a single layer.

Spoon the honey, the Worcestershire sauce, Chinese five spice powder with the soy sauce, sherry and chilli sauce into a small saucepan and heat gently, stirring until smooth. Stir in the chopped garlic, the tomato purée and mustard powder, if using.

Pour the honey mixture over ribs and spoon over until the ribs are coated evenly. Cover with clingfilm and leave to marinate overnight in the refrigerator, occasionally spooning the marinade over the ribs.

When ready to cook, remove the ribs from the marinade and place in a shallow roasting tin. Spoon over a little of the marinade and reserve the remainder. Place the spareribs in the preheated oven and cook for 35–40 minutes, or until cooked and the outsides are crisp. Baste occasionally with the reserved marinade during cooking. Garnish with a few spring onion curls and serve immediately, either as a starter or as a meat accompaniment.

Try this: FOR AN ALTERNATIVE: 64   FOR A MAIN COURSE: 226

Potato Skins

SERVES 4

4 large baking potatoes
2 tbsp olive oil
2 tsp paprika
125 g/4 oz pancetta,
    roughly chopped

6 tbsp double cream
125 g/4 oz Gorgonzola
    cheese
1 tbsp freshly
    chopped parsley

To serve:
mayonnaise
sweet chilli dipping sauce
tossed green salad

Preheat the oven to 200°C/400°F/Gas Mark 6. Scrub the potatoes, then prick a few times with a fork or skewer and place directly on the top shelf of the oven. Bake in the preheated oven for at least 1 hour, or until tender. The potatoes are cooked when they yield gently to the pressure of your hand.

Set the potatoes aside until cool enough to handle, then cut in half and scoop the flesh into a bowl and reserve. Preheat the grill and line the grill rack with tinfoil.

Mix together the oil and the paprika and use half to brush the outside of the potato skins. Place on the grill rack under the preheated hot grill and cook for 5 minutes, or until crisp, turning as necessary.

Heat the remaining paprika-flavoured oil and gently fry the pancetta until crisp. Add to the potato flesh along with the cream, Gorgonzola cheese and parsley. Halve the potato skins and fill with the Gorgonzola filling. Return to the oven for a further 15 minutes to heat through. Sprinkle with a little more paprika and serve immediately with mayonnaise, sweet chilli sauce and a green salad.

Try this: FOR AN ALTERNATIVE: 58   FOR A MAIN COURSE: 262

Winter Coleslaw

SERVES 6

175 g/6 oz white cabbage
1 medium red onion, peeled
175 g/6 oz carrot, peeled
175 g/6 oz celeriac, peeled
2 celery stalks, trimmed
75 g/3 oz golden sultanas

**For the yogurt &
  herb dressing:**
150 ml/¼ pint natural yogurt
1 garlic clove, peeled
  and crushed
1 tbsp lemon juice

1 tsp clear honey
1 tbsp freshly snipped
  chives

Remove the hard core from the cabbage with a small knife and shred finely. Slice the onion finely and coarsely grate the carrot. Place the raw vegetables in a large bowl and mix together.

Cut the celeriac into thin strips and simmer in boiling water for about 2 minutes. Drain the celeriac and rinse thoroughly with cold water.

Chop the celery and add to the bowl with the celeriac and sultanas and mix well.

Make the yogurt and herb dressing by briskly whisking the yogurt, garlic, lemon juice, honey and chives together.

Pour the dressing over the top of the salad. Stir the vegetables thoroughly to coat evenly and serve.

Try this: FOR AN ALTERNATIVE: 34   FOR A MAIN COURSE: 188

Fish & Shellfish

Traditional Fish Pie

SERVES 4

450 g/1 lb cod or coley fillets, skinned
450 ml/¾ pint milk
1 small onion, peeled and quartered
salt and freshly ground black pepper

900 g/2 lb potatoes, peeled and cut into chunks
100 g/3½ oz butter
125 g/4 oz large prawns
2 large eggs, hard-boiled and quartered
198 g can sweetcorn,

drained
2 tbsp freshly chopped parsley
3 tbsp plain flour
50 g/2 oz Cheddar cheese, grated

Preheat the oven to 200°C/400°F/Gas Mark 6, about 15 minutes before cooking. Place the fish in a shallow frying pan, pour over 300 ml/½ pint of the milk and add the onion. Season to taste with salt and pepper. Bring to the boil and simmer for 8–10 minutes until the fish is cooked. Remove the fish with a slotted spoon and place in a 1.4 litre/2½ pint baking dish. Strain the cooking liquid and reserve.

Boil the potatoes until soft, then mash with 40 g/1½ oz of the butter and 2–3 tablespoons of the remaining milk. Reserve.

Arrange the prawns and sliced eggs on top of the fish, then scatter over the sweetcorn and sprinkle with the parsley.

Melt the remaining butter in a saucepan, stir in the flour and cook gently for 1 minute, stirring. Whisk in the reserved cooking liquid and remaining milk. Cook for 2 minutes, or until thickened, then pour over the fish mixture and cool slightly.

Spread the mashed potato over the top of the pie and sprinkle over the grated cheese. Bake in the preheated oven for 30 minutes until golden. Serve immediately.

Try this: FOR AN ALTERNATIVE: 78   FOR A MEAT OR POULTRY OPTION: 122

Fish Lasagne

SERVES 4

75 g/3 oz mushrooms
1 tsp sunflower oil
1 small onion, peeled and
    finely chopped
1 tbsp freshly
    chopped oregano
400 g can chopped tomatoes
1 tbsp tomato purée
salt and freshly ground

black pepper
450 g/1 lb cod or haddock
    fillets, skinned
9–12 sheets pre-cooked
    lasagne verde

For the topping:
1 medium egg, beaten
125 g/4 oz cottage cheese

150 ml/¼ pint natural
    yoghurt
50 g/2 oz Cheddar cheese,
    grated

To serve:
mixed salad leaves
cherry tomatoes

Preheat the oven to 190°C/375°F/Gas Mark 5. Wipe the mushrooms, trim the stalks and chop. Heat the oil in a large heavy-based pan, add the onion and gently cook the onion for 3–5 minutes or until soft. Stir in the mushrooms, the oregano and the chopped tomatoes with their juice. Blend the tomato purée with 1 tablespoon of water. Stir into the pan and season to taste with salt and pepper. Bring the sauce to the boil, then simmer uncovered for 5–10 minutes.

Remove as many of the tiny pin bones as possible from the fish and cut into cubes and add to the tomato sauce mixture. Stir gently and remove the pan from the heat.

Cover the base of an ovenproof dish with 2–3 sheets of the lasagne verde. Top with half of the fish mixture. Repeat the layers finishing with the lasagne sheets.

To make the topping, mix together the beaten egg, cottage cheese and yoghurt. Pour over the lasagne and sprinkle with the cheese.

Cook the lasagne in the preheated oven for 40–45 minutes or until the topping is golden brown and bubbling. Serve the lasagne immediately with the mixed salad leaves and cherry tomatoes.

Try this: FOR AN ALTERNATIVE: 106   FOR A MEAT OR POULTRY OPTION: 170

Fish Crumble

SERVES 6

450 g/1 lb whiting or halibut
   fillets
300 ml/½ pint milk
salt and freshly ground
   black pepper
1 tbsp sunflower oil
75 g/3 oz butter or
   margarine
1 medium onion, peeled and
   finely chopped

2 leeks, trimmed and sliced
1 medium carrot, peeled and
   cut into small dice
2 medium potatoes, peeled
   and cut into small pieces
75 g/6 oz plain flour
300 ml/½ pint fish or
   vegetable stock
2 tbsp whipping cream
1 tsp freshly chopped dill

runner beans, to serve

For the crumble topping:
75 g/3 oz butter or
   margarine
175 g/6 oz plain flour
75 g/3 oz Parmesan
   cheese, grated
¾ tsp cayenne pepper

Preheat the oven to 200°C/400°F/Gas Mark 6, 15 minutes before cooking. Oil a 1.4 litre/2½ pint pie dish. Place the fish in a saucepan with the milk, salt and pepper. Bring to the boil, cover and simmer for 8–10 minutes until the fish is cooked. Remove with a slotted spoon, reserving the cooking liquid. Flake the fish into the prepared dish.

Heat the oil and 1 tablespoon of the butter or margarine in a small frying pan and gently fry the onion, leeks, carrot and potatoes for 1–2 minutes. Cover tightly and cook over a gentle heat for a further 10 minutes until softened. Spoon the vegetables over the fish.

Melt the remaining butter or margarine in a saucepan, add the flour and cook for 1 minute, stirring. Whisk in the reserved cooking liquid and the stock. Cook until thickened, then stir in the cream. Remove from the heat and stir in the dill. Pour over the fish.

To make the crumble, rub the butter or margarine into the flour until it resembles bread-crumbs, then stir in the cheese and cayenne pepper. Sprinkle over the dish, and bake in the preheated oven for 20 minutes until piping hot. Serve with runner beans.

Try this: FOR AN ALTERNATIVE: 74   FOR A MEAT OR POULTRY OPTION: 204

Foil-baked Fish

SERVES 4

For the tomato sauce:
125 ml/4 fl oz olive oil
4 garlic cloves, peeled and finely chopped
4 shallots, peeled and finely chopped
400 g can chopped Italian tomatoes

2 tbsp freshly chopped flat-leaf parsley
3 tbsp basil leaves
salt and freshly ground black pepper

700 g/1½ lb red mullet, bass or haddock fillets

450 g/1 lb live mussels
4 squids
8 large raw prawns
2 tbsp olive oil
3 tbsp dry white wine
3 tbsp freshly chopped basil leaves
lemon wedges, to garnish

Preheat oven to 180°C/350°F/Gas Mark 4, 10 minutes before cooking. Heat the olive oil and gently fry the garlic and shallots for 2 minutes. Stir in the tomatoes and simmer for 10 minutes, breaking the tomatoes down with the wooden spoon. Add the parsley and basil, season to taste with salt and pepper and cook for a further 2 minutes. Reserve and keep warm.

Lightly rinse the fish fillets and cut into 4 portions. Scrub the mussels thoroughly, removing the beard and any barnacles from the shells. Discard any mussels that are open. Clean the squid and cut into rings. Peel the prawns and remove the thin black intestinal vein that runs down the back.

Cut 4 large pieces of tinfoil, then place them on a large baking sheet and brush with olive oil. Place 1 fish portion in the centre of each piece of tinfoil. Close the tinfoil to form parcels and bake in the preheated oven for 10 minutes, then remove.

Carefully open up the parcels and add the mussels, squid and prawns. Pour in the wine and spoon over a little of the tomato sauce. Sprinkle with the basil leaves and return to the oven and bake for 5 minutes, or until cooked thoroughly. Disgard any unopened mussels, then garnish with lemon wedges and serve with the extra tomato sauce.

Try this: FOR AN ALTERNATIVE: 104   FOR A MEAT OR POULTRY OPTION: 208

Smoked Mackerel & Potato Salad

SERVES 4

½ tsp dry mustard powder
1 large egg yolk
salt and freshly ground
    black pepper
150 ml/¼ pint sunflower oil
1–2 tbsp lemon juice

450 g/1 lb baby new
    potatoes
25 g/1 oz butter
350 g/12 oz smoked
    mackerel fillets
4 celery stalks, trimmed and

    finely chopped
3 tbsp creamed horseradish
150 ml/¼ pint crème fraîche
1 Little Gem, rinsed and
    roughly torn
8 cherry tomatoes, halved

Place the mustard powder and egg yolk in a small bowl with salt and pepper and whisk until blended. Add the oil, drop by drop, into the egg mixture, whisking continuously. When the mayonnaise is thick, add the lemon juice, drop by drop, until a smooth, glossy consistency is formed. Reserve.

Cook the potatoes in boiling salted water until tender, then drain. Cool slightly, then cut into halves or quarters, depending on size. Return to the saucepan and toss in the butter.

Remove the skin from the mackerel fillets and flake into pieces. Add to the potatoes in the saucepan, together with the celery.

Blend 4 tablespoons of the mayonnaise with the horseradish and crème fraîche. Season to taste with salt and pepper, then add to the potato and mackerel mixture and stir lightly.

Arrange the lettuce and tomatoes on 4 serving plates. Pile the smoked mackerel mixture on top of the lettuce, grind over a little pepper and serve with the remaining mayonnaise.

Try this: FOR AN ALTERNATIVE: 112   FOR A MEAT OR POULTRY OPTION: 124

Ratatouille Mackerel

SERVES 4

1 red pepper
1 tbsp olive oil
1 red onion, peeled
1 garlic clove, peeled and
   thinly sliced
2 courgettes, trimmed and

cut into thick slices
400 g can chopped tomatoes
sea salt and freshly ground
   black pepper
4 x 275 g/10 oz small
   mackerel, cleaned and

heads removed
spray of olive oil
lemon juice for drizzling
12 fresh basil leaves
couscous or rice mixed with
   chopped parsley, to serve

Preheat the oven to 190°C/375°F/Gas Mark 5. Cut the top off the red pepper, remove the seeds and membrane, then cut into chunks. Cut the red onion into thick wedges.

Heat the oil in a large pan and cook the onion and garlic for 5 minutes or until beginning to soften.

Add the pepper chunks and courgette slices and cook for a further 5 minutes.

Pour in the chopped tomatoes with their juice and cook for a further 5 minutes. Season to taste with salt and pepper and pour into an ovenproof dish.

Season the fish with salt and pepper and arrange on top of the vegetables. Spray with a little olive oil and lemon juice. Cover and cook in the preheated oven for 20 minutes.

Remove the cover, add the basil leaves and return to the oven for a further 5 minutes. Serve immediately with couscous or rice mixed with parsley.

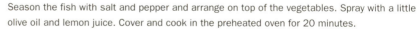 *Try this:* FOR AN ALTERNATIVE: 82   FOR A MEAT OR POULTRY OPTION: 146

Smoked Haddock Rosti

SERVES 4

450 g/1 lb potatoes, peeled
and coarsely grated
1 large onion, peeled and
coarsely grated
2–3 garlic cloves, peeled
and crushed
450 g/1 lb smoked haddock

1 tbsp olive oil
salt and freshly ground
black pepper
finely grated rind of
½ lemon
1 tbsp freshly
chopped parsley

2 tbsp half-fat crème fraîche
mixed salad leaves,
to garnish
lemon wedges, to serve

Dry the grated potatoes in a clean tea towel. Rinse the grated onion thoroughly in cold water, dry in a clean tea towel and add to the potatoes.

Stir the garlic into the potato mixture. Skin the smoked haddock and remove as many of the tiny pin bones as possible. Cut into thin slices and reserve.

Heat the oil in a non-stick frying pan. Add half the potatoes and press well down in the frying pan. Season to taste with salt and pepper.

Add a layer of fish and a sprinkling of lemon rind, parsley and a little black pepper.

Top with the remaining potatoes and press down firmly. Cover with a sheet of tinfoil and cook on the lowest heat for 25–30 minutes.

Preheat the grill 2–3 minutes before the end of cooking time. Remove the tinfoil and place the rosti under the grill to brown. Turn out on to a warmed serving dish, and serve immediately with spoonfuls of crème fraîche, lemon wedges and mixed salad leaves.

Try this: FOR AN ALTERNATIVE: 90   FOR A MEAT OR POULTRY OPTION: 120

Smoked Haddock Kedgeree

SERVES 4

450 g/1 lb smoked
  haddock fillets
50 g/2 oz butter
1 onion, peeled and
  finely chopped
2 tsp mild curry powder

175 g/6 oz long-grain rice
450 ml/¾ pint fish or
  vegetable stock, heated
2 large eggs, hard-boiled
  and shelled
2 tbsp freshly

chopped parsley
2 tbsp whipping cream
  (optional)
salt and freshly ground
  black pepper
pinch of cayenne pepper

Place the haddock in a shallow frying pan and cover with 300 ml/½ pint water. Simmer gently for 8–10 minutes, or until the fish is cooked. Drain, then remove all the skin and bones from the fish and flake into a dish. Keep warm.

Melt the butter in a saucepan and add the chopped onion and curry powder. Cook, stirring, for 3–4 minutes, or until the onion is soft, then stir in the rice. Cook for a further minute, stirring continuously, then stir in the hot stock.

Cover and simmer gently for 15 minutes, or until the rice has absorbed all the liquid. Cut the eggs into quarters or eighths and add half to the mixture with half the parsley.

Carefully fold in the cooked fish to the mixture and add the cream, if using. Season to taste with salt and pepper. Heat the kedgeree through briefly until piping hot.

Transfer the mixture to a large dish and garnish with the remaining quartered eggs, parsley and serve with a pinch of cayenne pepper. Serve immediately.

Try this: FOR AN ALTERNATIVE: 110   FOR A MEAT OR POULTRY OPTION: 198

Smoked Haddock Tart

SERVES 4

For the shortcut pastry:
150 g/5 oz plain flour
pinch of salt
25 g/1 oz lard or white
    vegetable fat, cut into
    small cubes
40 g/1½ oz butter or hard
    margarine, cut into
    small cubes

For the filling:
225 g/8 oz smoked haddock,
    skinned and cubed
2 large eggs, beaten
300 ml/½ pint double cream
1 tsp Dijon mustard
freshly ground black pepper
125 g/4 oz Gruyère
    cheese, grated

1 tbsp freshly
    snipped chives

To serve:
lemon wedges
tomato wedges
fresh green salad leaves

Preheat the oven to 190°C/375°F/Gas Mark 5. Sift the flour and salt into a large bowl. Add the fats and mix lightly. Using the fingertips rub into the flour until the mixture resembles breadcrumbs. Sprinkle 1 tablespoon of cold water into the mixture and with a knife, start bringing the dough together. (It may be necessary to use the hands for the final stage.) If the dough does not form a ball instantly, add a little more water. Put the pastry in a polythene bag and chill for at least 30 minutes.

On a lightly floured surface, roll out the pastry and use to line an 18 cm/7 inch lightly oiled quiche or flan tin. Prick the base all over with a fork and bake blind in the preheated oven for 15 minutes.

Carefully remove the pastry from the oven, brush with a little of the beaten egg. Return to the oven for a further 5 minutes, then place the fish in the pastry case.

For the filling, beat together the eggs and cream. Add the mustard, black pepper and cheese and pour over the fish. Sprinkle with the chives and bake for 35–40 minutes or until the filling is golden brown and set in the centre. Serve hot or cold with the lemon and tomato wedges and salad leaves.

Try this: FOR AN ALTERNATIVE: 88   FOR A MEAT OR POULTRY OPTION: 200

Salmon Fish Cakes

SERVES 4

225 g/8 oz potatoes, peeled
450 g/1 lb salmon
    fillet, skinned
125 g/4 oz carrot, trimmed
    and peeled
2 tbsp grated lemon rind

2–3 tbsp freshly
    chopped coriander
1 medium egg yolk
salt and freshly ground
    black pepper
2 tbsp plain white flour

few fine sprays of oil

To serve:
prepared tomato sauce
tossed green salad
crusty bread

Cube the potatoes and cook in lightly salted boiling water for 15 minutes. Drain and mash the potatoes. Place in a mixing bowl and reserve.

Place the salmon in a food processor and blend to form a chunky purée. Add the purée to the potatoes and mix together.

Coarsely grate the carrot and add to the fish with the lemon rind and the coriander.

Add the egg yolk, season to taste with salt and pepper, then gently mix the ingredients together. With damp hands form the mixture into 4 large fish cakes.

Coat in the flour and place on a plate. Cover loosely and chill for at least 30 minutes.

When ready to cook, spray a griddle pan with a few fine sprays of oil and heat the pan. When hot add the fish cakes and cook on both sides for 3–4 minutes or until the fish is cooked. Add an extra spray of oil if needed during the cooking.

When the fish cakes are cooked, serve immediately with the tomato sauce, green salad and crusty bread.

Try this: FOR AN ALTERNATIVE: 108   FOR A MEAT OR POULTRY OPTION: 192

Salmon with Herbed Potatoes

SERVES 4

450 g/1 lb baby new potatoes
salt and freshly ground black
   pepper
4 salmon steaks, each
   weighing about 175 g/6 oz
1 carrot, peeled and cut

into fine strips
175 g/6 oz asparagus spears,
   trimmed
175 g/6 oz sugar snap
   peas, trimmed
finely grated rind and juice

of 1 lemon
25 g/1 oz butter
4 large sprigs of fresh
   parsley

Preheat the oven to 190°C/375°F/Gas Mark 5, about 10 minutes before required. Parboil the potatoes in lightly salted boiling water for 5–8 minutes until they are barely tender. Drain and reserve.

Cut out 4 pieces of baking parchment paper, measuring 20.5 cm/8 inches square, and place on the work surface. Arrange the parboiled potatoes on top. Wipe the salmon steaks and place on top of the potatoes.

Place the carrot strips in a bowl with the asparagus spears, sugar snaps and grated lemon rind and juice. Season to taste with salt and pepper. Toss lightly together.

Divide the vegetables evenly between the salmon. Dot the top of each parcel with butter and a sprig of parsley.

To wrap a parcel, lift up 2 opposite sides of the paper and fold the edges together. Twist the paper at the other 2 ends to seal the parcel well. Repeat with the remaining parcels.

Place the parcels on a baking tray and bake in the preheated oven for 15 minutes. Place an unopened parcel on each plate and open just before eating.

Try this: FOR AN ALTERNATIVE: 82   FOR A MEAT OR POULTRY OPTION: 124

Smoked Salmon Quiche

SERVES 6

225 g/8 oz plain flour
50 g/2 oz butter
50 g/2 oz white vegetable
   fat or lard
2 tsp sunflower oil
225 g/8 oz potato, peeled
   and diced

125 g/4 oz Gruyère cheese,
   grated
75 g/3 oz smoked salmon
   trimmings
5 medium eggs, beaten
300 ml/½ pint single cream
salt and freshly ground

black pepper
1 tbsp freshly chopped
   flat-leaf parsley

To serve:
mixed salad
baby new potatoes

Preheat the oven to 200°C/400°F/Gas Mark 6. Blend the flour, butter and white vegetable fat or lard together until it resembles fine breadcrumbs. Blend again, adding sufficient water to make a firm but pliable dough. Use the dough to line a 23 cm/9 inch flan dish or tin, then chill the pastry case in the refrigerator for 30 minutes. Bake blind with baking beans for 10 minutes.

Heat the oil in a small frying pan, add the diced potato and cook for 3–4 minutes until lightly browned. Reduce the heat and cook for 2–3 minutes, or until tender. Leave to cool.

Scatter the grated cheese evenly over the base of the pastry case, then arrange the cooled potato on top. Add the smoked salmon in an even layer.

Beat the eggs with the cream and season to taste with salt and pepper. Whisk in the parsley and pour the mixture carefully into the dish.

Reduce the oven to 180°C/350°F/Gas Mark 4 and bake for about 30–40 minutes, or until the filling is set and golden. Serve hot or cold with a mixed salad and baby new potatoes.

Try this: FOR AN ALTERNATIVE: 92   FOR A MEAT OR POULTRY OPTION: 202

Citrus–grilled Plaice

SERVES 4

1 tsp sunflower oil
1 onion, peeled
   and chopped
1 orange pepper, deseeded
   and chopped
175 g/6 oz long-grain rice
150 ml/¼ pint orange juice

2 tbsp lemon juice
225 ml/8 fl oz vegetable stock
spray of oil
4 x 175 g/6 oz plaice
   fillets, skinned
1 orange
1 lemon

25 g/1 oz butter or
   margarine
2 tbsp freshly
   chopped tarragon
salt and freshly ground
   black pepper
lemon wedges, to garnish

Heat the oil in a large frying pan, then sauté the onion, pepper and rice for 2 minutes.

Add the orange and lemon juice and bring to the boil. Reduce the heat, add half the stock and simmer for 15–20 minutes, or until the rice is tender, adding the remaining stock as necessary.

Preheat the grill. Finely spray the base of the grill pan with oil. Place the plaice fillets in the base and reserve.

Finely grate the orange and lemon rind. Squeeze the juice from half of each fruit.

Melt the butter or margarine in a small saucepan. Add the grated rind, juice and half of the tarragon and use to baste the plaice fillets.

Cook one side only of the fish under the preheated grill at a medium heat for 4–6 minutes, basting continuously.

Once the rice is cooked, stir in the remaining tarragon and season to taste with salt and pepper. Garnish the fish with the lemon wedges and serve immediately with the rice

Try this: FOR AN ALTERNATIVE: 80   FOR A MEAT OR POULTRY OPTION: 178

Chunky Halibut Casserole

SERVES 4

50 g/2 oz butter or
  margarine
2 large onions, peeled and
  sliced into rings
1 red pepper, deseeded and
  roughly chopped
450 g/1 lb potatoes, peeled
450 g/1 lb courgettes,

  trimmed and thickly sliced
2 tbsp plain flour
1 tbsp paprika
2 tsp vegetable oil
300 ml/½ pint white wine
150 ml/¼ pint fish stock
400 g can chopped tomatoes
2 tbsp freshly chopped basil

salt and freshly ground
  black pepper
450 g/1 lb halibut fillet,
  skinned and cut into 2.5
  cm/1 inch cubes
sprigs of fresh basil,
  to garnish
freshly cooked rice, to serve

Melt the butter or margarine in a large saucepan, add the onions and pepper and cook for 5 minutes, or until softened.

Cut the peeled potatoes into 2.5 cm/1 inch dice, rinse lightly and shake dry, then add them to the onions and pepper in the saucepan. Add the courgettes and cook, stirring frequently, for a further 2–3 minutes.

Sprinkle the flour, paprika and vegetable oil into the saucepan and cook, stirring continuously, for 1 minute. Pour in 150 ml/¼ pint of the wine, with all the stock and the chopped tomatoes, and bring to the boil.

Add the basil to the casserole, season to taste with salt and pepper and cover. Simmer for 15 minutes, then add the halibut and the remaining wine and simmer very gently for a further 5–7 minutes, or until the fish and vegetables are just tender. Garnish with basil sprigs and serve immediately with freshly cooked rice.

Try this: FOR AN ALTERNATIVE: 78   FOR A MEAT OR POULTRY OPTION: 166

Battered Cod & Chunky Chips

SERVES 4

15 g/½ oz fresh yeast
300 ml/½ pint beer
225 g/8 oz plain flour
1 tsp salt
700 g/1½ lb potatoes
450 ml/¾ pint groundnut oil

4 cod fillets, about 225 g/8 oz
each, skinned and boned
2 tbsp seasoned plain flour

To garnish:
lemon wedges

sprigs of flat-leaf parsley

To serve:
tomato ketchup
vinegar

Dissolve the yeast with a little of the beer in a jug and mix to a paste. Pour in the remaining beer, whisking all the time until smooth. Place the flour and salt in a bowl, and gradually pour in the beer mixture, whisking continuously to make a thick smooth batter. Cover the bowl and allow the batter to stand at room temperature for 1 hour.

Peel the potatoes and cut into thick slices. Cut each slice lengthways to make chunky chips. Place them in a non-stick frying pan and heat, shaking the pan until all the moisture has evaporated. Turn them onto absorbent kitchen paper to dry off.

Heat the oil to 180°C/350°F, then fry the chips a few at a time for 4–5 minutes until crisp and golden. Drain on absorbent kitchen paper and keep warm.

Pat the cod fillets dry, then coat in the flour. Dip the floured fillets into the reserved batter. Fry for 2–3 minutes until cooked and crisp, then drain. Garnish with lemon wedges and parsley and serve immediately with the chips, tomato ketchup and vinegar.

Try this: FOR AN ALTERNATIVE: 106FOR A MEAT OR POULTRY OPTION: 168

Gingered Cod Steaks

SERVES 4

2.5 cm/1 inch piece fresh
   root ginger, peeled
4 spring onions
2 tsp freshly chopped

parsley
1 tbsp soft brown sugar
4 x 175 g/6 oz thick cod steaks
salt and freshly ground

black pepper
25 g/1 oz butter
freshly cooked vegetables,
   to serve

Preheat the grill and line the grill rack with a layer of tinfoil. Coarsely grate the piece of ginger. Trim the spring onions and cut into thin strips.

Mix the spring onions, ginger, chopped parsley and sugar. Add 1 tablespoon of water.

Wipe the fish steaks. Season to taste with salt and pepper. Place on to 4 separate 20.5 x 20.5 cm/8 x 8 inch tinfoil squares.

Carefully spoon the spring onions and ginger mixture over the fish. Cut the butter into small cubes and place over the fish.

Loosely fold the foil over the steaks to enclose the fish and to make a parcel. Place under the preheated grill and cook for 10–12 minutes or until cooked and the flesh has turned opaque.

Place the fish parcels on individual serving plates. Serve immediately with the freshly cooked vegetables.

Try this: FOR AN ALTERNATIVE: 80   FOR A MEAT OR POULTRY OPTION: 244

Saucy Cod & Pasta Bake

SERVES 4

450 g/1 lb cod fillets, skinned
2 tbsp sunflower oil
1 onion, peeled and chopped
4 rashers smoked streaky bacon, rind removed and chopped
150 g/5 oz baby button mushrooms, wiped

2 celery sticks, trimmed and thinly sliced
2 small courgettes, halved lengthwise and sliced
400 g can chopped tomatoes
100 ml/3½ fl oz fish stock or dry white wine
1 tbsp freshly chopped tarragon

salt and freshly ground black pepper

For the pasta topping:
225–275 g/8–10 oz pasta shells
25 g/1 oz butter
4 tbsp plain flour
450 ml/¾ pint milk

Preheat the oven to 200°C/400°F/Gas Mark 6, 15 minutes before cooking. Cut the cod into bite-sized pieces and reserve.

Heat the sunflower oil in a large saucepan, add the onion and bacon and cook for 7–8 minutes. Add the mushrooms and celery and cook for 5 minutes, or until fairly soft. Add the courgettes and tomatoes to the bacon mixture and pour in the fish stock or wine. Bring to the boil, then simmer uncovered for 5 minutes, or until the sauce has thickened slightly.

Remove from the heat and stir in the cod pieces and the tarragon. Season to taste with salt and pepper, then spoon into a large oiled baking dish. Meanwhile, bring a large pan of lightly salted water to a rolling boil. Add the pasta shells and cook, according to the packet instructions, or until 'al dente'.

For the topping, place the butter and flour in a saucepan and pour in the milk. Bring to the boil slowly, whisking until thickened and smooth. Drain the pasta thoroughly, and stir into the sauce. Spoon carefully over the fish and vegetables. Place in the preheated oven and bake for 20–25 minutes, or until the top is lightly browned and bubbling.

Try this: FOR AN ALTERNATIVE: 102   FOR A MEAT OR POULTRY OPTION: 218

Tuna Fish Burgers

MAKES 8

450 g/1 lb potatoes, peeled
   and cut into chunks
50 g/2 oz butter
2 tbsp milk
400 g can tuna in oil
1 spring onion, trimmed and
   finely chopped
1 tbsp freshly chopped

parsley
salt and freshly ground
   black pepper
2 medium eggs, beaten
2 tbsp seasoned plain flour
125 g/4 oz fresh white
   breadcrumbs
4 tbsp vegetable oil

4 sesame seed baps
   (optional)

To serve:
fat chips
mixed salad
tomato chutney

Place the potatoes in a large saucepan, cover with boiling water and simmer until soft. Drain, then mash with 40 g/1½ oz of the butter and the milk. Turn into a large bowl. Drain the tuna, discarding the oil and flake into the bowl of potato. Stir well to mix.

Add the spring onions and parsley to the mixture and season to taste with salt and pepper. Add 1 tablespoon of the beaten egg to bind the mixture together. Chill in the refrigerator for at least 1 hour.

Shape the chilled mixture with your hands into 4 large burgers. First, coat the burgers with seasoned flour, then brush them with the remaining beaten egg, allowing any excess to drip back into the bowl. Finally, coat them evenly in the breadcrumbs, pressing the crumbs on with your hands, if necessary.

Heat a little of the oil in a frying pan and fry the burgers for 2–3 minutes on each side until golden, adding more oil if necessary. Drain on absorbent kitchen paper and serve hot in baps, if using, with chips, mixed salad and chutney.

Try this: FOR AN ALTERNATIVE: 92   FOR A MEAT OR POULTRY OPTION: 192

Paella

SERVES 4

450 g/1 lb live mussels
4 tbsp olive oil
6 medium chicken thighs
1 medium onion, peeled and
   finely chopped
1 garlic clove, peeled and
   crushed
225 g/8 oz tomatoes,
   skinned, deseeded
   and chopped

1 red pepper, deseeded
   and chopped
1 green pepper, deseeded
   and chopped
125 g/4 oz frozen peas
1 tsp paprika
450 g/1 lb Arborio rice
½ tsp turmeric
900 ml/1½ pints chicken
   stock, warmed

175 g/6 oz large
   peeled prawns
salt and freshly ground
   black pepper
2 limes
1 lemon
1 tbsp freshly chopped basil
whole cooked unpeeled
   prawns, to garnish

Rinse the mussels under cold running water, scrubbing well to remove any grit and barnacles, then pull off the hairy 'beards'. Tap any open mussels sharply with a knife, and discard if they refuse to close. Heat the oil in a paella pan or large, heavy-based frying pan and cook the chicken thighs for 10–15 minutes until golden. Remove and keep warm. Fry the onion and garlic in the remaining oil in the pan for 2–3 minutes, then add the tomatoes, peppers, peas and paprika and cook for a further 3 minutes.

Add the rice to the pan and return the chicken with the turmeric and half the stock. Bring to the boil and simmer, gradually adding more stock as it is absorbed. Cook for 20 minutes, or until most of the stock has been absorbed and the rice is almost tender.

Put the mussels in a large saucepan with 5 cm/2 inches boiling salted water, cover and steam for 5 minutes. Discard any with shells that have not opened, then stir into the rice with the prawns. Season to taste with salt and pepper. Heat through for 2–3 minutes until piping hot. Squeeze the juice from 1 of the limes over the paella. Cut the remaining limes and the lemon into wedges and arrange on top of the paella. Sprinkle with the basil, garnish with the prawns and serve.

Try this: FOR AN ALTERNATIVE: 88 FOR A MEAT OR POULTRY OPTION: 194

Supreme Baked Potatoes

SERVES 4

4 large baking potatoes
40 g/1½ oz butter
1 tbsp sunflower oil
1 carrot, peeled and
 chopped

2 celery stalks, trimmed and
 finely chopped
200 g can white crab meat
2 spring onions, trimmed
 and finely chopped

salt and freshly ground
 black pepper
50 g/2 oz Cheddar cheese,
 grated
tomato salad, to serve

Preheat the oven to 200°C/400°F/Gas Mark 6. Scrub the potatoes and prick all over with a fork, or thread 2 potatoes onto 2 long metal skewers. Place the potatoes in the preheated oven for 1–1½ hours, or until soft to the touch. Allow to cool a little, then cut in half.

Scoop out the cooked potato and turn into a bowl, leaving a reasonably firm potato shell. Mash the cooked potato flesh, then mix in the butter and mash until the butter has melted.

While the potatoes are cooking, heat the oil in a frying pan and cook the carrot and celery for 2 minutes. Cover the pan tightly and continue to cook for another 5 minutes, or until the vegetables are tender.

Add the cooked vegetables to the bowl of mashed potato and mix well. Fold in the crab meat and the spring onions, then season to taste with salt and pepper.

Pile the mixture back into the potato shells and press in firmly. Sprinkle the grated cheese over the top and return the potato halves to the oven for 12–15 minutes until hot, golden and bubbling. Serve immediately with a tomato salad.

Try this: FOR AN ALTERNATIVE: 82   FOR A MEAT OR POULTRY OPTION: 168

Cheesy Vegetable & Prawn Bake

SERVES 4

175 g/6 oz long-grain rice
salt and freshly ground
   black pepper
1 garlic clove, peeled
   and crushed
1 large egg, beaten
3 tbsp freshly shredded basil

4 tbsp Parmesan cheese,
   grated
125 g/4 oz baby asparagus
   spears, trimmed
150 g/5 oz baby carrots,
   trimmed
150 g/5 oz fine green

beans, trimmed
150 g/5 oz cherry tomatoes
175 g/6 oz peeled prawns,
   thawed if frozen
125 g/4 oz mozzarella
   cheese, thinly sliced

Preheat the oven to 200°C/400°F/Gas Mark 6, about 10 minutes before required. Cook the rice in lightly salted boiling water for 12–15 minutes, or until tender, drain. Stir in the garlic, beaten egg, shredded basil, 2 tablespoons of the Parmesan cheese and season to taste with salt and pepper. Press this mixture into a greased 23 cm/9 inch square ovenproof dish and reserve.

Bring a large saucepan of water to the boil, then drop in the asparagus, carrots and green beans. Return to the boil and cook for 3–4 minutes. Drain and leave to cool.

Quarter or halve the cherry tomatoes and mix them into the cooled vegetables. Spread the prepared vegetables over the rice and top with the prawns. Season to taste with salt and pepper.

Cover the prawns with the mozzarella and sprinkle over the remaining Parmesan cheese. Bake in the preheated oven for 20–25 minutes until piping hot and golden brown in places. Serve immediately.

Try this: FOR AN ALTERNATIVE: 76   FOR A MEAT OR POULTRY OPTION: 218

Mussels Linguine

SERVES 4

2 kg/4½ lb fresh mussels,
    washed and scrubbed
knob of butter
1 onion, peeled and
    finely chopped
300 ml/½ pint medium dry
    white wine

For the sauce:
1 tbsp sunflower oil
4 baby onions, peeled
    and quartered
2 garlic cloves, peeled
    and crushed
400 g can chopped tomatoes

large pinch of salt
225 g/8 oz dried linguine
    or tagliatelle
2 tbsp freshly chopped
    parsley

Soak the mussels in plenty of cold water. Leave in the refrigerator until required. When ready to use, scrub the mussel shells, removing any barnacles or beards. Discard any open mussels.

Melt the butter in a large pan. Add the mussels, onion and wine. Cover with a close-fitting lid and steam for 5–6 minutes, shaking the pan gently to ensure even cooking. Discard any mussels that have not opened, then strain and reserve the liquor.

To make the sauce, heat the oil in a medium-sized saucepan, and gently fry the quartered onion and garlic for 3–4 minutes until soft and transparent. Stir in the tomatoes and half the reserved mussel liquor. Bring to the boil and simmer for 7–10 minutes until the sauce begins to thicken.

Cook the pasta in boiling salted water for 7 minutes or or until 'al dente'. Drain the pasta, reserving 2 tablespoons of the cooking liquor, then return the pasta and liquor to the pan.

Remove the meat from half the mussel shells. Stir into the sauce along with the remaining mussels. Pour the hot sauce over the cooked pasta and toss gently. Garnish with the parsley and serve immediately.

Try this: FOR AN ALTERNATIVE: 110   FOR A MEAT OR POULTRY OPTION: 220

Meat

Lancashire Hotpot

SERVES 4

1 kg/2¼ lb middle end neck of
    lamb, divided into cutlets
2 tbsp vegetable oil
2 large onions, peeled
    and sliced
2 tsp plain flour
150 ml/¼ pint vegetable

or lamb stock
700 g/1½ lb waxy potatoes,
    peeled and thickly sliced
salt and freshly ground
    black pepper
1 bay leaf
2 sprigs of fresh thyme

1 tbsp melted butter
2 tbsp freshly chopped
    herbs, to garnish
freshly cooked green beans,
    to serve

Preheat the oven to 170°C/325°F/Gas Mark 3. Trim any excess fat from the lamb cutlets. Heat the oil in a frying pan and brown the cutlets in batches for 3–4 minutes. Remove with a slotted spoon and reserve. Add the onions to the frying pan and cook for 6–8 minutes until softened and just beginning to colour, then remove and reserve.

Stir in the flour and cook for a few seconds, then gradually pour in the stock, stirring well, and bring to the boil. Remove from the heat.

Spread the base of a large casserole with half the potato slices. Top with half the onions and season well with salt and pepper. Arrange the browned meat in a layer. Season again and add the remaining onions, bay leaf and thyme. Pour in the remaining liquid from the onions and top with remaining potatoes so that they overlap in a single layer. Brush the potatoes with the melted butter and season again.

Cover the saucepan and cook in the preheated oven for 2 hours, uncovering for the last 30 minutes to allow the potatoes to brown. Garnish with chopped herbs and serve immediately with green beans.

Try this: FOR AN ALTERNATIVE: 140   FOR A POULTRY OR VEGETABLE OPTION: 208

Shepherd's Pie

SERVES 4

2 tbsp vegetable or olive oil
1 onion, peeled and
  finely chopped
1 carrot, peeled and
  finely chopped
1 celery stalk, trimmed
  and finely chopped
1 tbsp sprigs of fresh thyme

450 g/1 lb leftover roast
  lamb, finely chopped
150 ml/¼ pint red wine
150 ml/¼ pint lamb or
  vegetable stock or
  leftover gravy
2 tbsp tomato purée
salt and freshly ground

black pepper
700 g/1½ lb potatoes, peeled
  and cut into chunks
25 g/1 oz butter
6 tbsp milk
1 tbsp freshly chopped parsley
fresh herbs, to garnish

Preheat the oven to 200°C/400°F/Gas Mark 6, about 15 minutes before cooking. Heat the oil in a large saucepan and add the onion, carrot and celery. Cook over a medium heat for 8–10 minutes until softened and starting to brown.

Add the thyme and cook briefly, then add the cooked lamb, wine, stock and tomato purée. Season to taste with salt and pepper and simmer gently for 25–30 minutes until reduced and thickened. Remove from the heat to cool slightly and season again.

Meanwhile, boil the potatoes in plenty of salted water for 12–15 minutes until tender. Drain and return to the saucepan over a low heat to dry out. Remove from the heat and add the butter, milk and parsley. Mash until creamy, adding a little more milk if necessary. Adjust the seasoning.

Transfer the lamb mixture to a shallow ovenproof dish. Spoon the mash over the filling and spread evenly to cover completely. Fork the surface, place on a baking sheet, then cook in the preheated oven for 25–30 minutes until the potato topping is browned and the filling is piping hot. Garnish and serve.

 Try this: FOR AN ALTERNATIVE: 120   FOR A POULTRY OR VEGETABLE OPTION: 204

Roast Leg of Lamb & Boulangère Potatoes

SERVES 6

1.1 kg/2½ lb potatoes, peeled
1 large onion, peeled
    and finely sliced
salt and freshly ground
    black pepper
2 tbsp olive oil

50 g/2 oz butter
200 ml/7 fl oz lamb stock
100 ml/3½ fl oz milk
2 kg/4½ lb leg of lamb
2–3 sprigs of fresh rosemary
6 large garlic cloves, peeled

    and finely sliced
6 anchovy fillets, drained
extra sprigs of fresh
    rosemary, to garnish

Preheat the oven to 230°C/450°F/Gas Mark 8. Finely slice the potatoes – a mandolin is the best tool for this. Layer the potatoes with the onion in a large roasting tin, seasoning each layer with salt and pepper. Drizzle about 1 tablespoon of the olive oil over the potatoes and add the butter in small pieces. Pour in the lamb stock and milk and reserve.

Make small incisions all over the lamb with the point of a small, sharp knife. Into each incision insert a small piece of rosemary, a sliver of garlic and a piece of anchovy fillet.

Drizzle the leg of lamb and its flavourings with the rest of the olive oil and season well. Place the meat directly on to a shelf in the preheated oven. Position the roasting tin of potatoes directly underneath to catch the juices during cooking. Roast for 15 minutes per 500 g/1 lb 2 oz (about 1 hour for a joint this size), reducing the oven temperature after 20 minutes to 200°C/400°F/Gas Mark 6.

When the lamb is cooked, remove from the oven and allow to rest for 10 minutes before carving. Meanwhile, increase the oven heat and cook the potatoes for a further 10–15 minutes to crisp up. Garnish with fresh rosemary sprigs and serve immediately with the lamb.

Try this: FOR AN ALTERNATIVE: 126   FOR A POULTRY OR VEGETABLE OPTION: 212

Leg of Lamb with Minted Rice

SERVES 4

1 tbsp olive oil
1 medium onion, peeled
   and finely chopped
1 garlic clove, peeled
   and crushed
1 celery stalk, trimmed

and chopped
1 large mild red chilli,
   deseeded and chopped
75 g/3 oz long-grain rice
150 ml/¼ pint lamb or
   chicken stock

2 tbsp freshly chopped mint
salt and freshly ground
   black pepper
1.4 kg/3 lb boned leg of lamb
freshly cooked vegetables,
   to serve

Preheat the oven to 190°C/375°F/Gas Mark 5, 10 minutes before roasting. Heat the oil in a frying pan and gently cook the onion for 5 minutes. Stir in the garlic, celery and chilli and continue to cook for 3–4 minutes.

Place the rice and the stock in a large saucepan and cook, covered, for 10–12 minutes or until the rice is tender and all the liquid is absorbed. Stir in the onion and celery mixture, then leave to cool. Once the rice mixture is cold, stir in the chopped mint and season to taste with salt and pepper.

Place the boned lamb skin-side down and spoon the rice mixture along the centre of the meat. Roll up the meat to enclose the stuffing and tie securely with string. Place in a roasting tin and roast in the preheated oven for 1 hour 20 minutes, or until cooked to personal preference. Remove from the oven and leave to rest in a warm place for 20 minutes, before carving. Serve with a selection of cooked vegetables.

Try this: FOR AN ALTERNATIVE: 128   FOR A POULTRY OR VEGETABLE OPTION: 210

Crown Roast of Lamb

SERVES 6

1 lamb crown roast
salt and freshly ground
   black pepper
1 tbsp sunflower oil
1 small onion, peeled and
   finely chopped
2–3 garlic cloves, peeled
   and crushed

2 celery stalks, trimmed
   and finely chopped
125 g/4 oz cooked mixed
   basmati and wild rice
75 g/3 oz ready-to-eat-dried
   apricots, chopped
50 g/2 oz pine nuts, toasted
1 tbsp finely grated

orange rind
2 tbsp freshly chopped
   coriander
1 small egg, beaten
freshly roasted potatoes and
   green vegetables, to serve

Preheat the oven to 180°C/350°F/Gas Mark 4, about 10 minutes before roasting. Wipe the crown roast and season the cavity with salt and pepper. Place in a roasting tin and cover the ends of the bones with small pieces of foil.

Heat the oil in a small saucepan and cook the onion, garlic and celery for 5 minutes, then remove the saucepan from the heat. Add the cooked rice with the apricots, pine nuts, orange rind and coriander. Season with salt and pepper, then stir in the egg and mix well.

Carefully spoon the prepared stuffing into the cavity of the lamb, then roast in the preheated oven for 1–1½ hours. Remove the lamb from the oven and remove and discard the foil from the bones. Return to the oven and continue to cook for a further 15 minutes, or until cooked to personal preference.

Remove from the oven and leave to rest for 10 minutes before serving with the roast potatoes and freshly cooked vegetables.

Try this: FOR AN ALTERNATIVE: 130   FOR A POULTRY OR VEGETABLE OPTION: 208

Roasted Lamb with Rosemary & Garlic

SERVES 6

1.6 kg/3½ lb leg of lamb
8 garlic cloves, peeled
few sprigs of fresh rosemary
salt and freshly ground
    black pepper

4 slices pancetta
4 tbsp olive oil
4 tbsp red wine vinegar
900 g/2 lb potatoes
1 large onion

sprigs of fresh rosemary,
    to garnish
freshly cooked ratatouille,
    to serve

Preheat oven to 200°C/400°F/Gas Mark 6, 15 minutes before roasting. Wipe the leg of lamb with a clean damp cloth, then place the lamb in a large roasting tin. With a sharp knife, make small, deep incisions into the meat. Cut 2–3 garlic cloves into small slivers, then insert with a few small sprigs of rosemary into the lamb. Season to taste with salt and pepper and cover the lamb with the slices of pancetta.

Drizzle over 1 tablespoon of the olive oil and lay a few more rosemary sprigs across the lamb. Roast in the preheated oven for 30 minutes, then pour over the vinegar.

Peel the potatoes and cut into large dice. Peel the onion and cut into thick wedges then thickly slice the remaining garlic. Arrange around the lamb. Pour the remaining olive oil over the potatoes, then reduce the oven temperature to 180°C/350°F/Gas Mark 4 and roast for a further 1 hour, or until the lamb is tender. Garnish with fresh sprigs of rosemary and serve immediately with the roast potatoes and ratatouille.

Try this: FOR AN ALTERNATIVE: 134   FOR A POULTRY OR VEGETABLE OPTION: 256

Braised Lamb with Broad Beans

SERVES 4

700 g/1½ lb lamb, cut into
   large chunks
1 tbsp plain flour
1 onion
2 garlic cloves
1 tbsp olive oil

400 g can chopped tomatoes
   with basil
300 ml/½ pint lamb stock
2 tbsp freshly chopped thyme
2 tbsp freshly
   chopped oregano

salt and freshly ground
   black pepper
150 g/5 oz frozen broad beans
fresh oregano, to garnish
creamy mashed potatoes,
   to serve

Trim the lamb, discarding any fat or gristle, then place the flour in a polythene bag, add the lamb and toss until coated thoroughly. Peel and slice the onion and garlic and reserve. Heat the olive oil in a heavy-based saucepan and when hot, add the lamb and cook, stirring, until the meat is sealed and browned all over. Using a slotted spoon transfer the lamb to a plate and reserve.

Add the onion and garlic to the saucepan and cook for 3 minutes, stirring frequently until softened, then return the lamb to the saucepan. Add the chopped tomatoes with their juice, the stock, the chopped thyme and oregano to the pan and season to taste with salt and pepper. Bring to the boil, then cover with a close-fitting lid, reduce the heat and simmer for 1 hour.

Add the broad beans to the lamb and simmer for 20–30 minutes, or until the lamb is tender. Garnish with fresh oregano and serve with creamy mashed potatoes.

Try this: FOR AN ALTERNATIVE: 140   FOR A POULTRY OR VEGETABLE OPTION: 214

Marinated Lamb Chops with Garlic Fried Potatoes

SERVES 4

4 thick lamb chump chops
3 tbsp olive oil
550 g/1¼ lb potatoes,
    peeled and cut into
    1 cm/½ inch dice
6 unpeeled garlic cloves
mixed salad or freshly cooked

vegetables, to serve

For the marinade:
1 small bunch of fresh
    thyme, leaves removed
1 tbsp freshly
    chopped rosemary

1 tsp salt
2 garlic cloves, peeled
    and crushed
rind and juice of 1 lemon
2 tbsp olive oil

Trim the chops of any excess fat, wipe with a clean damp cloth and reserve. To make the marinade, using a pestle and mortar, pound the thyme leaves and rosemary with the salt until pulpy. Add the garlic and continue pounding until crushed. Stir in the lemon rind and juice and the olive oil.

Pour the marinade over the lamb chops, turning them until they are well coated. Cover lightly and leave to marinate in the refrigerator for about 1 hour.

Meanwhile, heat the oil in a large non-stick frying pan. Add the potatoes and garlic and cook over a low heat for about 20 minutes, stirring occasionally. Increase the heat and cook for a further 10–15 minutes until golden. Drain on absorbent kitchen paper and add salt to taste. Keep warm.

Heat a griddle pan until almost smoking. Add the lamb chops and cook for 3–4 minutes on each side until golden, but still pink in the middle. Serve with the potatoes, and either a mixed salad or freshly cooked vegetables.

Try this: FOR AN ALTERNATIVE: 136   FOR A POULTRY OR VEGETABLE OPTION: 256

Brandied Lamb Chops

SERVES 4

8 lamb loin chops
3 tbsp groundnut oil
5 cm/2 inch piece fresh root
   ginger, peeled and cut
   into matchsticks
2 garlic cloves, peeled
   and chopped
225 g/8 oz button mushrooms,
wiped, and halved if large
2 tbsp light soy sauce
2 tbsp dry sherry
1 tbsp brandy
1 tsp Chinese five-
   spice powder
1 tsp soft brown sugar
200 ml/7 fl oz lamb or
chicken stock
1 tsp sesame oil

To serve:
freshly cooked rice
freshly stir-fried vegetables

Using a sharp knife, trim the lamb chops, discarding any sinew or fat. Heat a wok or large frying pan, add the oil and when hot, add the lamb chops and cook for 3 minutes on each side or until browned. Using a fish slice, transfer the lamb chops to a plate and keep warm.

Add the ginger, garlic and button mushrooms to the wok and stir-fry for 3 minutes or until the mushrooms have browned.

Return the lamb chops to the wok together with the soy sauce, sherry, brandy, five-spice powder and sugar. Pour in the stock, bring to the boil, then reduce the heat slightly and simmer for 4–5 minutes, or until the lamb is tender, ensuring that the liquid does not evaporate completely. Add the sesame oil and heat for a further 30 seconds. Turn into a warmed serving dish and serve immediately with freshly cooked rice and stir-fried vegetables.

Try this: FOR AN ALTERNATIVE: 134   FOR A POULTRY OR VEGETABLE OPTION: 202

Lamb's Liver
with Bacon & Onions

SERVES 4

350 g/12 oz lamb's liver
2 heaped tbsp plain flour
salt and freshly ground
    black pepper
2 tbsp groundnut oil
2 large onions, peeled
    and finely sliced
2 garlic cloves, peeled

and chopped
1 red chilli, deseeded
    and chopped
175 g/6 oz streaky bacon
40 g/1½ oz butter
300 ml/½ pint lamb
    or beef stock
2 tbsp freshly

chopped parsley

To serve:
freshly cooked creamy
    mashed potatoes
freshly cooked green
    vegetables
freshly cooked carrots

Trim the liver, discarding any sinew or tubes, and thinly slice. Season the flour with salt and pepper, then use to coat the liver and reserve.

Heat a wok, then add the oil and when hot, add the sliced onion, garlic and chilli and cook for 5–6 minutes, or until soft and browned. Remove from the wok with a slotted spoon and reserve. Cut each slice of the bacon in half and stir-fry for 3–4 minutes or until cooked. Remove with a slotted spoon and add to the onions.

Melt the butter in the wok and fry the liver on all sides until browned and crisp. Pour in the stock and allow to bubble fiercely for 1–2 minutes. Return the onions and bacon to the wok, stir thoroughly, then cover. Simmer gently for 10 minutes, or until the liver is tender. Sprinkle with the parsley and serve immediately with mashed potatoes and green vegetables and carrots.

Try this: FOR AN ALTERNATIVE: 164   FOR A POULTRY OR VEGETABLE OPTION: 200

Pork Chop Hotpot

SERVES 4

4 pork chops
flour for dusting
225 g/8 oz shallots, peeled
2 garlic cloves, peeled
50 g/2 oz sun-dried tomatoes
2 tbsp olive oil
400 g can plum tomatoes

150 ml/¼ pint red wine
150 ml/¼ pint chicken stock
3 tbsp tomato purée
2 tbsp freshly
   chopped oregano
salt and freshly ground
   black pepper

fresh oregano leaves,
   to garnish

To serve:
freshly cooked new potatoes
French beans

Preheat oven to 190˚C/375˚F/Gas Mark 5, 10 minutes before cooking. Trim the pork chops, removing any excess fat, wipe with a clean, damp cloth, then dust with a little flour and reserve. Cut the shallots in half if large. Chop the garlic and slice the sun-dried tomatoes.

Heat the olive oil in a large casserole and cook the pork chops for about 5 minutes, turning occasionally during cooking, until browned all over. Using a slotted spoon, carefully lift out of the dish and reserve. Add the shallots and cook for 5 minutes, stirring occasionally.

Return the pork chops to the casserole and scatter with the garlic and sun-dried tomatoes, then pour over the can of tomatoes with their juice.

Blend the red wine, stock and tomato purée together and add the chopped oregano. Season to taste with salt and pepper, then pour over the pork chops and bring to a gentle boil. Cover with a close-fitting lid and cook in the preheated oven for 1 hour, or until the pork chops are tender. Adjust the seasoning to taste, then scatter with a few oregano leaves and serve immediately with freshly cooked potatoes and French beans.

Try this: FOR AN ALTERNATIVE: 120   FOR A POULTRY OR VEGETABLE OPTION: 236

Pork Sausages with Onion Gravy & Best–ever Mash

SERVES 4

50 g/2 oz butter
1 tbsp olive oil
2 large onions, peeled
    and thinly sliced
pinch of sugar
1 tbsp freshly
    chopped thyme
1 tbsp plain flour

100 ml/3½ fl oz Madeira
200 ml/7 fl oz vegetable stock
8–12 good-quality butchers'
    pork sausages, depending
    on size

For the mash:
900 g/2 lb floury potatoes,
    peeled
75 g/3 oz butter
4 tbsp crème fraîche or
    soured cream
salt and freshly ground
    black pepper

Melt the butter with the oil and add the onions. Cover and cook gently for about 20 minutes until the onions have collapsed. Add the sugar and stir well. Uncover and continue to cook, stirring often, until the onions are very soft and golden. Add the thyme, stir well, then add the flour, stirring. Gradually add the Madeira and the stock. Bring to the boil and simmer gently for 10 minutes.

Meanwhile, put the sausages in a large frying pan and cook over a medium heat for about 15–20 minutes, turning often, until golden brown and slightly sticky all over.

For the mash, boil the potatoes in plenty of lightly salted water for 15–18 minutes until tender. Drain well and return to the saucepan. Put the saucepan over a low heat to allow the potatoes to dry thoroughly. Remove from the heat and add the butter, crème fraîche (or soured cream) and salt and pepper. Mash thoroughly. Serve the potato mash topped with the sausages and onion gravy.

 Try this: FOR AN ALTERNATIVE: 144   FOR A POULTRY OR VEGETABLE OPTION: 264

Oven–roasted Vegetables with Sausages

SERVES 4

2 medium aubergines, trimmed
3 medium courgettes, trimmed
4 tbsp olive oil

6 garlic cloves, peeled
8 Tuscany-style sausages
4 plum tomatoes
2 x 300 g cans cannellini beans
salt and freshly ground

black pepper
1 bunch of fresh basil, torn into coarse pieces
4 tbsp Parmesan cheese, grated

Preheat oven to 200°C/400°F/Gas Mark 6, 15 minutes before cooking. Cut the aubergines and courgettes into bite-sized chunks. Place the olive oil in a large roasting tin and heat in the preheated oven for 3 minutes, or until very hot. Add the aubergines, courgettes and garlic cloves, then stir until coated in the hot oil and cook in the oven for 10 minutes.

Remove the roasting tin from the oven and stir. Lightly prick the sausages, add to the roasting tin and return to the oven. Continue to roast for a further 20 minutes, turning once during cooking, until the vegetables are tender and the sausages are golden brown.

Meanwhile, roughly chop the plum tomatoes and drain the cannellini beans. Remove the sausages from the oven and stir in the tomatoes and cannellini beans. Season to taste with salt and pepper, then return to the oven for 5 minutes, or until heated thoroughly.

Scatter over the basil leaves and sprinkle with plenty of Parmesan cheese and extra freshly ground black pepper. Serve immediately.

Try this: FOR AN ALTERNATIVE: 142   FOR A POULTRY OR VEGETABLE OPTION: 256

Leek & Ham Risotto

SERVES 4

1 tbsp olive oil
25 g/1 oz butter
1 medium onion, peeled
   and finely chopped
4 leeks, trimmed and
   thinly sliced

1½ tbsp freshly
   chopped thyme
350 g/12 oz Arborio rice
1.4 litres/2¼ pints vegetable
   or chicken stock, heated
225 g/8 oz cooked ham

175 g/6 oz peas, thawed
   if frozen
50 g/2 oz Parmesan
   cheese, grated
salt and freshly ground
   black pepper

Heat the oil and half the butter together in a large saucepan. Add the onion and leeks and cook over a medium heat for 6–8 minutes, stirring occasionally, until soft and beginning to colour. Stir in the thyme and cook briefly.

Add the rice and stir well. Continue stirring over a medium heat for about 1 minute until the rice is glossy. Add a ladleful or two of the stock and stir well until the stock is absorbed. Continue adding stock, a ladleful at a time, and stirring well between additions, until about two thirds of the stock has been added.

Meanwhile, either chop or finely shred the ham, then add to the saucepan of rice together with the peas. Continue adding ladlefuls of stock, as described in step 2, until the rice is tender and the ham is heated through thoroughly.

Add the remaining butter, sprinkle over the Parmesan cheese and season to taste with salt and pepper. When the butter has melted and the cheese has softened, stir well to incorporate. Taste and adjust the seasoning, then serve immediately.

 Try this: FOR AN ALTERNATIVE: 162   FOR A POULTRY OR VEGETABLE OPTION: 254

Roast Cured Pork Loin with Baked Sliced Potatoes

SERVES 4

2 tbsp wholegrain mustard
2 tbsp clear honey
1 tsp coarsely crushed
   black pepper
900 g/2 lb piece smoked
   cured pork loin

900 g/2 lb potatoes, peeled
   and thinly sliced
75 g/3 oz butter, diced
1 large onion, peeled and
   finely chopped
25 g/1 oz plain flour

salt and freshly ground
   black pepper
600 ml/1 pint milk
fresh green salad, to serve

Preheat the oven to 190°C/375°F/Gas Mark 5. Mix together the mustard, honey and black pepper. Spread evenly over the pork loin. Place in the centre of a large square of foil and wrap loosely. Cook in the preheated oven for 15 minutes per 450 g/1 lb, plus an extra 15 minutes (45 minutes), unwrapping the joint for the last 30 minutes of cooking time.

Meanwhile, layer one third of the potatoes, one third of the butter, half the onions and half the flour in a large gratin dish. Add half the remaining potatoes and butter and the remaining onions and flour. Finally, cover with the remaining potatoes. Season well with salt and pepper between layers. Pour in the milk and dot with the remaining butter. Cover the dish loosely with foil and put in the oven below the pork. Cook for 1½ hours.

Remove the foil from the potatoes and cook for a further 20 minutes until tender and golden. Remove the pork loin from the oven and leave to rest for 10 minutes before carving thinly. Serve with the potatoes and a fresh green salad.

Try this: FOR AN ALTERNATIVE: 150   FOR A POULTRY OR VEGETABLE OPTION: 206

Pork Loin Stuffed with Orange & Hazelnut Rice

SERVES 4

15 g/½ oz butter
1 shallot, peeled and
    finely chopped
50 g/2 oz long-grain brown rice
175 ml/6 fl oz vegetable stock
½ orange
25 g/1 oz ready-to-eat

dried prunes, stoned
    and chopped
25 g/1 oz hazelnuts, roasted
    and roughly chopped
1 small egg, beaten
1 tbsp freshly chopped parsley
salt and freshly ground black

pepper
450 g/1 lb boneless pork
    tenderloin or fillet, trimmed

To serve:
steamed courgettes
carrots

Preheat the oven to 190°C/375°F/Gas Mark 5, 10 minutes before required. Heat the butter in a small saucepan, add the shallot and cook gently for 2–3 minutes until softened. Add the rice and stir well for 1 minute. Add the stock, stir well and bring to the boil. Cover tightly and simmer gently for 30 minutes until the rice is tender and all the liquid is absorbed. Leave to cool.

Grate the orange rind and reserve. Remove the white pith and chop the orange flesh finely. Mix together the orange rind and flesh, prunes, hazelnuts, cooled rice, egg and parsley. Season to taste with salt and pepper.

Cut the fillet in half, then using a sharp knife, split the pork fillet lengthways almost in two, forming a pocket, leaving it just attached. Open out the pork and put between 2 pieces of clingfilm. Flatten using a meat mallet until about half its original thickness. Spoon the filling into the pocket and close the fillet over. Tie along the length with kitchen string at regular intervals.

Put the pork fillet in a small roasting tray and cook in the top of the preheated oven for 25–30 minutes, or until the meat is just tender. Remove from the oven and allow to rest for 5 minutes. Slice into rounds and serve with steamed courgettes and carrots.

Try this: FOR AN ALTERNATIVE: 148   FOR A POULTRY OR VEGETABLE OPTION: 210

Pork Meatballs with Vegetables

SERVES 4

450 g/1 lb pork mince
2 tbsp freshly
    chopped coriander
2 garlic cloves, peeled
    and chopped
1 tbsp light soy sauce
salt and freshly ground
    black pepper
2 tbsp groundnut oil

2.5 cm/1 inch piece fresh
    root ginger, peeled and
    cut into matchsticks
1 red pepper, deseeded
    and cut into chunks
1 green pepper, deseeded
    and cut into chunks
2 courgettes, trimmed
    and cut into sticks

125 g/4 oz baby sweetcorn,
    halved lengthways
3 tbsp light soy sauce
1 tsp sesame oil
fresh coriander leaves,
    to garnish
freshly cooked noodles,
    to serve

Mix together the pork mince, the chopped coriander, half the garlic and the soy sauce, then season to taste with salt and pepper. Divide into 20 portions and roll into balls. Place on a baking sheet, cover with clingfilm and chill in the refrigerator for at least 30 minutes.

Heat a wok or large frying pan, add the groundnut oil and when hot, add the meatballs and cook for 8–10 minutes, or until the pork balls are browned all over, turning occasionally. Using a slotted spoon, transfer the balls to a plate and keep warm.

Add the ginger and remaining garlic to the wok and stir-fry for 30 seconds. Add the red and green peppers and stir-fry for 5 minutes. Add the courgettes and sweetcorn and stir-fry for 3 minutes.

Return the pork balls to the wok, add the soy sauce and sesame oil and stir-fry for 1 minute, until heated through. Garnish with coriander leaves and serve immediately on a bed of noodles.

Try this: FOR AN ALTERNATIVE: 174   FOR A POULTRY OR VEGETABLE OPTION: 192

Cassoulet

SERVES 4

1 tbsp olive oil
1 onion, peeled and
   chopped
2 celery sticks, trimmed and
   chopped
175 g/6 oz carrots, peeled
   and sliced

2–3 garlic cloves,
   peeled and crushed
350 g/12 oz pork belly
   (optional)
8 spicy thick sausages, such
   as Toulouse
few sprigs of fresh thyme

salt and freshly ground
   black pepper
2 x 400 g/14 oz cans cannellini
   beans, drained and rinsed
600 ml/1 pint vegetable stock
75 g/3 oz fresh breadcrumbs
2 tbsp freshly chopped thyme

Preheat the oven to 180°C/350°F/Gas Mark 4. Heat the oil in a large saucepan or ovenproof casserole, add the onion, celery, carrot and garlic and cook for 5 minutes. Cut the pork, if using, into small pieces and cut the sausages into chunks.

Add the meat to the vegetables and cook, stirring, until lightly browned.

Add the thyme sprigs and season to taste with salt and pepper. If a saucepan was used, transfer everything to an ovenproof casserole.

Spoon the beans on top, then pour in the stock. Mix the breadcrumbs with 1 tablespoon of the chopped thyme in a small bowl and sprinkle on top of the beans. Cover with a lid and cook in the oven for 40 minutes. Remove the lid and cook for a further 15 minutes, or until the breadcrumbs are crisp. Sprinkle with the remaining chopped thyme and serve.

Try this: FOR AN ALTERNATIVE: 142   FOR A POULTRY OR VEGETABLE OPTION: 258

Pork with Assorted Peppers

SERVES 4

450 g/1 lb pork fillet
2 tbsp groundnut oil
1 onion, peeled and
    thinly sliced
1 red pepper, deseeded
    and cut into strips
1 yellow pepper, deseeded
    and cut into strips

1 orange pepper, deseeded
    and cut into strips
2 garlic cloves, peeled
    and crushed
2 tsp paprika
400 g can chopped tomatoes
300 ml/½ pint pork or
    chicken stock

1 tsp soft dark brown sugar
salt and freshly ground
    black pepper
handful fresh oregano leaves
350 g/12 oz penne
2 tbsp grated
    mozzarella cheese

Trim the pork fillet, discarding any sinew and fat, then cut into small cubes. Heat the wok, add the oil and when hot, stir-fry the pork for 3–4 minutes until they are brown and sealed. Remove the pork from the wok and reserve.

Add the sliced onions to the wok and stir-fry until they are softened, but not browned, then add the pepper strips and stir-fry for a further 3–4 minutes.

Stir in the garlic, paprika, chopped tomatoes, stock, sugar and seasoning and bring to the boil. Simmer, uncovered, stirring occasionally, for 15 minutes, or until the sauce has reduced and thickened. Return the pork to the wok and simmer for a further 5–10 minutes. Sprinkle with the oregano leaves.

Cook the pasta for 3–4 minutes until 'al dente' or according to packet directions, then drain and serve immediately with the pork and grated mozzarella cheese.

Try this: FOR AN ALTERNATIVE: 144   FOR A POULTRY OR VEGETABLE OPTION: 266

Bacon, Mushroom & Cheese Puffs

SERVES 4

1 tbsp olive oil
225 g/8 oz field mushrooms,
  wiped and roughly chopped
225 g/8 oz rindless streaky
  bacon, roughly chopped
2 tbsp freshly chopped parsley

salt and freshly ground
  black pepper
350 g/12 oz ready-rolled puff
  pastry sheets, thawed
  if frozen
25 g/1 oz Emmenthal

  cheese, grated
1 medium egg, beaten
salad leaves such as rocket
  or watercress, to garnish
tomatoes, to serve

Preheat the oven to 200˚C/400˚F/Gas Mark 6. Heat the olive oil in a large frying pan. Add the mushrooms and bacon and fry for 6–8 minutes until golden in colour. Stir in the parsley, season to taste with salt and pepper and allow to cool.

Roll the sheet of pastry a little thinner on a lightly floured surface to a 30.5 cm/12 inch square. Cut the pastry into 4 equal squares. Stir the grated Emmenthal cheese into the mushroom mixture. Spoon a quarter of the mixture on to one half of each square. Brush the edges of the square with a little of the beaten egg.

Fold over the pastry to form a triangular parcel. Seal the edges well and place on a lightly oiled baking sheet. Repeat until the squares are done.

Make shallow slashes in the top of the pastry with a knife. Brush the parcels with the remaining beaten egg and cook in the preheated oven for 20 minutes, or until puffy and golden brown.

Serve warm or cold, garnished with the salad leaves and served with tomatoes.

Try this: FOR AN ALTERNATIVE: 168 FOR A POULTRY OR VEGETABLE OPTION: 262

Cannelloni

SERVES 4

2 tbsp olive oil
175 g/6 oz fresh pork mince
75 g/3 oz chicken livers,
    chopped
1 small onion, peeled
    and chopped
1 garlic clove, peeled
    and chopped

175 g/6 oz frozen chopped
    spinach, thawed
1 tbsp freeze-dried oregano
pinch of freshly grated nutmeg
salt and freshly ground
    black pepper
175 g/6 oz ricotta cheese
25 g/1 oz butter

25 g/1 oz plain flour
600 ml/1 pint milk
600 ml/1 pint ready-made
    tomato sauce
16 precooked cannelloni tubes
50 g/2 oz Parmesan
    cheese, grated
green salad, to serve

Preheat oven to 190°C/375°F/Gas Mark 5, 10 minutes before cooking. Heat the olive oil in a frying pan and cook the mince and chicken livers for about 5 minutes, stirring occasionally, until browned all over. Break up any lumps if necessary with a wooden spoon.

Add the onion and garlic and cook for 4 minutes, until softened. Add the spinach, oregano and nutmeg and season to taste with salt and pepper. Cook until all the liquid has evaporated, then remove the pan from the heat and allow to cool. Stir in the ricotta cheese.

Meanwhile, melt the butter in a small saucepan and stir in the plain flour to form a roux. Cook for 2 minutes, stirring occasionally. Remove from the heat and blend in the milk until smooth. Return to the heat and bring to the boil, stirring until the sauce has thickened. Reserve.

Spoon a thin layer of the tomato sauce on the base of a large ovenproof dish. Divide the pork filling between the cannelloni tubes. Arrange on top of the tomato sauce. Spoon over the remaining tomato sauce.

Pour over the white sauce and sprinkle with the Parmesan cheese. Bake in the preheated oven for 30–35 minutes, or until the cannelloni is tender and the top is golden brown. Serve immediately with a green salad.

 Try this: FOR AN ALTERNATIVE: 170   FOR A POULTRY OR VEGETABLE OPTION: 274

Special Fried Rice

SERVES 4

25 g/1 oz butter
4 medium eggs, beaten
4 tbsp vegetable oil
1 bunch spring onions,
    trimmed and shredded
225 g/8 oz cooked ham, diced
125 g/4 oz large cooked

prawns with tails left on
75 g/3 oz peas, thawed
    if frozen
200 g can water chestnuts,
    drained and
    roughly chopped
450 g/1 lb cooked long-

grain rice
3 tbsp dark soy sauce
1 tbsp dry sherry
2 tbsp freshly chopped
    coriander
salt and freshly ground
    black pepper

Melt the butter in a wok or large frying pan and pour in half the beaten egg. Cook for 4 minutes drawing the edges of the omelette in to allow the uncooked egg to set into a round shape. Using a fish slice, lift the omelette from the wok and roll into a sausage shape. Leave to cool completely then using a sharp knife slice the omelette into rings.

Wipe the wok with absorbent kitchen paper and return to the heat. Add the oil and when hot, add the spring onions, ham, prawns, peas and chopped water chestnuts and stir-fry for 2 minutes. Add the rice and stir-fry for a further 3 minutes.

Add the remaining beaten eggs and stir-fry for 3 minutes, or until the egg has scrambled and set. Stir in the soy sauce, sherry and chopped coriander. Season to taste with salt and pepper and heat through thoroughly. Add the omelette rings and stir gently without breaking up the egg too much. Serve immediately.

Try this: FOR AN ALTERNATIVE: 146   FOR A POULTRY OR VEGETABLE OPTION: 282

Seared Calves' Liver with Onions & Mustard Mash

SERVES 2

2 tbsp olive oil
100 g/3½ oz butter
3 large onions, peeled
   and finely sliced
pinch of sugar
salt and freshly ground

black pepper
1 tbsp sprigs of fresh thyme
1 tbsp balsamic vinegar
700 g/1½ lb potatoes, peeled
   and cut into chunks
6–8 tbsp milk

1 tbsp wholegrain mustard
3–4 fresh sage leaves
550 g/1¼ lb thinly sliced
   calves' liver
1 tsp lemon juice

Preheat the oven to 150°C/300°F/Gas Mark 2. Heat half the oil and 25 g/1 oz of the butter in a flameproof casserole. When foaming, add the onions. Cover and cook over a low heat for 20 minutes until softened and beginning to collapse. Add the sugar and season with salt and pepper. Stir in the thyme. Cover the casserole and transfer to the preheated oven. Cook for a further 30–45 minutes until softened completely, but not browned. Remove from the oven and stir in the balsamic vinegar.

Meanwhile, boil the potatoes in boiling salted water for 15–18 minutes until tender. Drain well, then return to the pan. Place over a low heat to dry completely, remove from the heat and stir in 50 g/2 oz of the butter, the milk, mustard and salt and pepper to taste. Mash thoroughly until creamy and keep warm.

Heat a large frying pan and add the remaining butter and oil. When it is foaming, add the mustard and sage leaves and stir for a few seconds, then add the liver. Cook over a high heat for 1–2 minutes on each side. It should remain slightly pink: do not overcook. Remove the liver from the pan. Add the lemon juice to the pan and swirl around to deglaze.

To serve, place a large spoonful of the mashed potato on each plate. Top with some of the melting onions, the liver and finally the pan juices.

Try this: FOR AN ALTERNATIVE: 138   FOR A POULTRY OR VEGETABLE OPTION: 204

Steak & Kidney Stew

SERVES 4

1 tbsp olive oil
1 onion, peeled and
    chopped
2–3 garlic cloves,
    peeled and crushed
2 celery sticks,
    trimmed and sliced
550 g/1¼ lb braising steak,
    trimmed and diced
100 g/4 oz lambs' kidneys,

cored and chopped
2 tbsp plain flour
1 tbsp tomato purée
900 ml/1½ pints beef stock
salt and freshly ground
    black pepper
1 fresh bay leaf
300 g/10 oz carrots,
    peeled and sliced
350 g/12 oz baby new

potatoes, scrubbed
350 g/12 oz fresh spinach
    leaves, chopped

For the dumplings:
100 g/4 oz self-raising flour
50 g/2 oz shredded suet
1 tbsp freshly chopped
    mixed herbs
2–3 tbsp water

Heat the oil in a large, heavy-based saucepan, add the onion, garlic and celery and cook for 5 minutes, or until browned. Remove from the pan with a slotted spoon and reserve. Add the steak and kidneys to the pan and cook for 3–5 minutes, or until sealed, then return the onion mixture to the pan. Sprinkle in the flour and cook, stirring, for 2 minutes. Take off the heat, stir in the tomato purée, then the stock, and season to taste with salt and pepper. Add the bay leaf.

Return to the heat and bring to the boil, stirring occasionally. Add the carrots, then reduce the heat to a simmer and cover with a lid. Cook for 1¼ hours, stirring occasionally. Reduce the heat if the liquid is evaporating quickly. Add the potatoes and cook for a further 30 minutes.

Place the flour, suet and herbs in a bowl and add a little seasoning. Add the water and mix to a stiff mixture. Using a little extra flour, shape into 8 small balls. Place the dumplings on top of the stew, cover with the lid and continue to cook for 15 minutes, or until the meat is tender and the dumplings are well risen and fluffy. Stir in the spinach and leave to stand for 2 minutes, or until the spinach is wilted.

Try this: FOR AN ALTERNATIVE: 188   FOR A POULTRY OR VEGETABLE OPTION: 140

Cornish Pasties

SERVES 4

For the pastry:
350 g/12 oz self-raising flour
75 g/3 oz butter or margarine
75 g/3 oz lard or white
    vegetable fat
salt and freshly ground
    black pepper

For the filling:
550 g/1¼ lb braising steak,
    very finely chopped
1 large onion, peeled and
    finely chopped
1 large potato, peeled
    and diced
200 g/7 oz swede, peeled

and diced
3 tbsp Worcestershire sauce
1 small egg, beaten, to glaze

To garnish:
tomato slices or wedges
sprigs of fresh parsley

Preheat the oven to 180°C/350°F/Gas Mark 4, about 15 minutes before required. To make the pastry, sift the flour into a large bowl and add the fats, chopped into little pieces. Rub the fats and flour together until the mixture resembles coarse breadcrumbs. Season to taste with salt and pepper and mix again.

Add about 2 tablespoons of cold water, a little at a time, and mix until the mixture comes together to form a firm but pliable dough. Turn on to a lightly floured surface, knead until smooth, then wrap and chill in the refrigerator.

To make the filling, put the braising steak in a large bowl with the onion. Add the potatoes and swede to the bowl together with the Worcestershire sauce and salt and pepper. Mix well.

Divide the dough into 8 balls and roll each ball into a circle about 25.5 cm/10 inches across. Divide the filling between the circles of pastry. Wet the edge of the pastry, then fold over the filling. Pinch the edges to seal. Transfer the pasties to a lightly oiled baking sheet. Make a couple of small holes in each pasty and brush with beaten egg. Cook in the preheated oven for 15 minutes, remove and brush again with the egg. Return to the oven for a further 15–20 minutes until golden. Cool slightly, garnish with tomato and parsley and serve.

Try this: FOR AN ALTERNATIVE: 184   FOR A POULTRY OR VEGETABLE OPTION: 292

Traditional Lasagne

SERVES 4

450 g/1 lb lean minced beef steak

175 g/6 oz pancetta or smoked streaky bacon, chopped

1 large onion, peeled and chopped

2 celery stalks, trimmed and chopped

125 g/4 oz button mushrooms, wiped and chopped

2 garlic cloves, peeled and chopped

90 g/3½ oz plain flour

300 ml/½ pint beef stock

1 tbsp freeze-dried mixed herbs

5 tbsp tomato purée

salt and freshly ground black pepper

75 g/3 oz butter

1 tsp English mustard powder

pinch of freshly grated nutmeg

900 ml/1½ pints milk

125 g/4 oz Parmesan cheese, grated

125 g/4 oz Cheddar cheese, grated

8–12 precooked lasagne sheets

crusty bread, to serve

fresh green salad leaves, to serve

Preheat the oven to 200°C/400°F/Gas Mark 6, 15 minutes before cooking. Cook the beef and pancetta in a large saucepan for 10 minutes, stirring to break up any lumps. Add the onion, celery and mushrooms and cook for 4 minutes, or until softened slightly. Stir in the garlic and 1 tablespoon of the flour, then cook for 1 minute. Stir in the stock, herbs and tomato purée. Season to taste with salt and pepper. Bring to the boil, then cover, reduce the heat and simmer for 45 minutes.

Meanwhile, melt the butter in a small saucepan and stir in the remaining flour, mustard powder and nutmeg, until well blended. Cook for 2 minutes. Remove from the heat and gradually blend in the milk until smooth. Return to the heat and bring to the boil, stirring, until thickened. Gradually stir in half the Parmesan and Cheddar cheeses until melted. Season to taste.

Spoon half the meat mixture into the base of a large ovenproof dish. Top with a single layer of pasta. Spread over half the sauce and scatter with half the cheese. Repeat layers finishing with cheese. Bake in the preheated oven for 30 minutes, or until the pasta is cooked and the top is golden brown and bubbly. Serve immediately with crusty bread and a green salad.

Try this: FOR AN ALTERNATIVE: 172   FOR A POULTRY OR VEGETABLE OPTION: 240

Spaghetti Bolognese

SERVES 4

3 tbsp olive oil
50 g/2 oz unsmoked streaky
   bacon, rind removed
   and chopped
1 small onion, peeled
   and finely chopped
1 carrot, peeled and
   finely chopped

1 celery stalk, trimmed and
   finely chopped
2 garlic cloves, peeled
   and crushed
1 bay leaf
500 g/1 lb 2 oz minced
   beef steak
400 g can chopped tomatoes

2 tbsp tomato paste
150 ml/¼ pint red wine
150 ml/1⁄4 pint beef stock
salt and freshly gound
   black pepper
450 g/1 lb spaghetti
freshly grated Parmesan
   cheese, to serve

Heat the olive oil in a large heavy-based pan, add the bacon and cook for 5 minutes or until slightly coloured. Add the onion, carrot, celery, garlic and bay leaf and cook, stirring, for 8 minutes, or until the vegetables are soft.

Add the minced beef to the pan and cook, stirring with a wooden spoon to break up any lumps in the meat, for 5-8 minutes, or until browned.

Stir the tomatoes and tomato paste into the mince and pour in the wine and stock. Bring to the boil, lower the heat and simmer for at least 40 minutes, stirring occasionally. The longer you leave the sauce to cook, the more intense the flavour. Season to taste with salt and pepper and remove the bay leaf.

Meanwhile, bring a large pan of lightly salted water to a rolling boil, add the spaghetti and cook for about 8 minutes or until 'al dente'. Drain and arrange on warmed serving plates. Top with the prepared Bolognese sauce and serve immediately sprinkled with grated Parmesan cheese.

Try this: FOR AN ALTERNATIVE: 174   FOR A POULTRY OR VEGETABLE OPTION: 276

Spaghetti & Meatballs

SERVES 4

400 g can chopped tomatoes
1 tbsp tomato paste
1 tsp chilli sauce
¼ tsp brown sugar
salt and freshly ground
    black pepper
350 g/12 oz spaghetti
75g/3 oz Cheddar cheese,
    grated, plus extra to serve

freshly chopped parsley,
    to garnish

For the meatballs:
450 g/1 lb lean pork or
    beef mince
125 g/4 oz
    fresh breadcrumbs
1 large onion, peeled and

    finely chopped
1 medium egg, beaten
1 tbsp tomato paste
2 tbsp freshly chopped
    parsley
1 tbsp freshly
    chopped oregano

Preheat the oven to 200°C/400°F/Gas Mark 6, 15 minutes before using. Place the chopped tomatoes, tomato paste, chilli sauce and sugar in a saucepan. Season to taste with salt and pepper and bring to the boil. Cover and simmer for 15 minutes, then cook, uncovered, for a further 10 minutes, or until the sauce has reduced and thickened.

Meanwhile, make the meatballs. Place the meat, breadcrumbs and onion in a food processor. Blend until all the ingredients are well mixed. Add the beaten egg, tomato paste, parsley and oregano and season to taste. Blend again. Shape the mixture into small balls, about the size of an apricot, and place on an oiled baking tray. Cook in the preheated oven for 25–30 minutes, or until browned and cooked.

Meanwhile, bring a large pan of lightly salted water to a rolling boil. Add the pasta and cook according to the packet instructions, or until 'al dente'.

Drain the pasta and return to the pan. Pour over the tomato sauce and toss gently to coat the spaghetti. Tip into a warmed serving dish and top with the meatballs. Garnish with chopped parsley and serve immediately with grated cheese.

 Try this: FOR AN ALTERNATIVE: 152   FOR A POULTRY OR VEGETABLE OPTION: 220

Italian Beef Pot Roast

SERVES 6

1.8 kg/4 lb brisket of beef
225 g/8 oz small onions,
  peeled
3 garlic cloves, peeled
  and chopped
2 celery sticks, trimmed
  and chopped

2 carrots, peeled and sliced
450 g/1 lb ripe tomatoes
300 ml/½ pint Italian red wine
2 tbsp olive oil
300 ml/½ pint beef stock
1 tbsp tomato purée
2 tsp freeze-dried mixed herbs

salt and freshly ground
  black pepper
25 g/1 oz butter
25 g/1 oz plain flour
freshly cooked vegetables,
  to serve

Preheat oven to 150˚C/300˚F/Gas Mark 2, 10 minutes before cooking. Place the beef in a bowl. Add the onions, garlic, celery and carrots. Place the tomatoes in a bowl and cover with boiling water. Allow to stand for 2 minutes and drain. Peel away the skins, discard the seeds and chop, then add to the bowl with the red wine. Cover tightly and marinate in the refrigerator overnight.

Lift the marinated beef from the bowl and pat dry with absorbent kitchen paper. Heat the olive oil in a large casserole and cook the beef until it is browned all over, then remove from the dish. Drain the vegetables from the marinade, reserving the marinade. Add the vegetables to the casserole and fry gently for 5 minutes, stirring occasionally, until all the vegetables are browned.

Return the beef to the casserole with the marinade, beef stock, tomato purée and mixed herbs and season with salt and pepper. Bring to the boil, then cover and cook in the preheated oven for 3 hours.

Using a slotted spoon transfer the beef and any large vegetables to a plate and leave in a warm place. Blend the butter and flour to form a paste. Bring the casserole juices to the boil and then gradually stir in small spoonfuls of the paste. Cook until thickened. Serve with the sauce and a selection of vegetables.

Try this: FOR AN ALTERNATIVE: 166   FOR A POULTRY OR VEGETABLE OPTION: 214

Grilled Steaks with Saffron Potatoes & Roast Tomatoes

SERVES 4

700 g/1½ lb new potatoes, halved
few strands of saffron
300 ml/½ pint vegetable or beef stock
1 small onion, peeled and

finely chopped
75 g/3 oz butter
salt and freshly ground black pepper
2 tsp balsamic vinegar
2 tbsp olive oil

1 tsp caster sugar
8 plum tomatoes, halved
4 boneless sirloin steaks, each weighing 225 g/8 oz
2 tbsp freshly chopped parsley

Cook the potatoes in boiling salted water for 8 minutes and drain well. Return the potatoes to the saucepan along with the saffron, stock, onion and 25 g/1 oz of the butter. Season to taste with salt and pepper and simmer uncovered for 10 minutes until the potatoes are tender.

Meanwhile, preheat the grill to medium. Mix together the vinegar, olive oil, sugar and seasoning. Arrange the tomatoes cut-side up in a foil-lined grill pan and drizzle over the dressing. Grill for 12–15 minutes, basting occasionally, until tender.

Melt the remaining butter in a frying pan. Add the steaks and cook for 4–8 minutes to taste and depending on thickness.

Arrange the potatoes and tomatoes in the centre of 4 serving plates. Top with the steaks along with any pan juices. Sprinkle over the parsley and serve immediately.

Try this: FOR AN ALTERNATIVE: 180   FOR A POULTRY OR VEGETABLE OPTION: 264

Fillet Steaks with Tomato & Garlic Sauce

SERVES 4

700 g/1½ lb ripe tomatoes
2 garlic cloves
2 tbsp olive oil
2 tbsp freshly chopped basil
2 tbsp freshly

chopped oregano
2 tbsp red wine
salt and freshly ground
black pepper
75 g/3 oz pitted black

olives, chopped
4 fillet steaks, about 175 g/6
oz each in weight
freshly cooked vegetables,
to serve

Make a small cross on the top of each tomato and place in a large bowl. Cover with boiling water and leave for 2 minutes. Using a slotted spoon, remove the tomatoes and skin carefully. Repeat until all the tomatoes are skinned. Place on a chopping board, cut into quarters, remove the seeds and roughly chop, then reserve.

Peel and chop the garlic. Heat half the olive oil in a saucepan and cook the garlic for 30 seconds. Add the chopped tomatoes with the basil, oregano, red wine and season to taste with salt and pepper. Bring to the boil then reduce the heat, cover and simmer for 15 minutes, stirring occasionally, or until the sauce is reduced and thickened. Stir the olives into the sauce and keep warm while cooking the steaks.

Meanwhile, lightly oil a griddle pan or heavy-based frying pan with the remaining olive oil and cook the steaks for 2 minutes on each side to seal. Continue to cook the steaks for a further 2–4 minutes, depending on personal preference. Serve the steaks immediately with the garlic sauce and freshly cooked vegetables.

Try this: FOR AN ALTERNATIVE: 182   FOR A POULTRY OR VEGETABLE OPTION: 290

Pan–fried Beef with Creamy Mushrooms

SERVES 4

225 g/8 oz shallots, peeled
2 garlic cloves, peeled
2 tbsp olive oil
4 medallions of beef
4 plum tomatoes

125 g/4 oz flat mushrooms
3 tbsp brandy
150 ml/¼ pint red wine
salt and freshly ground
    black pepper

4 tbsp double cream

To serve:
baby new potatoes
freshly cooked green beans

Cut the shallots in half if large, then chop the garlic. Heat the oil in a large frying pan and cook the shallots for about 8 minutes, stirring occasionally, until almost softened. Add the garlic and beef and cook for 8–10 minutes, turning once during cooking until the meat is browned all over. Using a slotted spoon, transfer the beef to a plate and keep warm.

Rinse the tomatoes and cut into eighths, then wipe the mushrooms and slice. Add to the pan and cook for 5 minutes, stirring frequently until the mushrooms have softened.

Pour in the brandy and heat through. Draw the pan off the heat and carefully ignite. Allow the flames to subside. Pour in the wine, return to the heat and bring to the boil. Boil until reduced by one third. Draw the pan off the heat, season to taste with salt and pepper, add the cream and stir.

Arrange the beef on serving plates and spoon over the sauce. Serve with baby new potatoes and a few green beans.

Try this: FOR AN ALTERNATIVE: 178   FOR A POULTRY OR VEGETABLE OPTION: 238

Beef & Red Wine Pie

SERVES 4

175 g/6 oz ready-made quick
   flaky pastry, chilled
700 g/1½ lb stewing
   beef, cubed
4 tbsp seasoned plain flour
2 tbsp sunflower oil
2 onions, peeled and chopped

2 garlic cloves, peeled and
   crushed
1 tbsp freshly chopped
   thyme
300 ml/½ pint red wine
150 ml/¼ pint beef stock
1–2 tsp Worcestershire sauce

2 tbsp tomato ketchup
2 bay leaves
a knob of butter
225 g/8 oz button
   mushrooms
beaten egg or milk, to glaze
sprig of parsley, to garnish

Preheat the oven to 200°C/400°F/Gas Mark 6. Toss the beef cubes in the seasoned flour.

Heat the oil in a large heavy-based frying pan. Fry the beef in batches for about 5 minutes until golden brown. Return all of the beef to the pan and add the onions, garlic and thyme. Fry for about 10 minutes, stirring occasionally. If the beef begins to stick, add a little water.

Add the red wine and stock and bring to the boil. Stir in the Worcestershire sauce, tomato ketchup and bay leaves. Cover and simmer on a very low heat for about 1½ hours or until the beef is tender.

Heat the butter and gently sauté the mushrooms until golden brown. Add to the stew. Simmer uncovered for a further 15 minutes. Remove the bay leaves. Spoon the beef into a 1.1 litre/2 pint pie dish and reserve.

Roll out the pastry on a lightly floured surface. Cut out the lid to 5 mm/¼ inch wider than the dish. Brush the rim with the beaten egg and lay the pastry lid on top. Press to seal, then knock the edges with the back of the knife. Cut a slit in the lid and brush with the beaten egg or milk to glaze. Bake in the preheated oven for 30 minutes, or until golden brown. Garnish with the sprig of parsley and serve immediately.

 Try this: FOR AN ALTERNATIVE: 176   FOR A POULTRY OR VEGETABLE OPTION: 292

Chilli Con Carne with Crispy–skinned Potatoes

SERVES 4

2 tbsp vegetable oil, plus extra for brushing
1 large onion, peeled and finely chopped
1 garlic clove, peeled and finely chopped
1 red chilli, deseeded and finely chopped

450 g/1 lb chuck steak, finely chopped, or lean beef mince
1 tbsp chilli powder
400 g can chopped tomatoes
2 tbsp tomato purée
400 g can red kidney beans, drained and rinsed

4 large baking potatoes
coarse salt and freshly ground black pepper

To serve:
ready-made guacamole
soured cream

Preheat the oven to 150°C/300°F/Gas Mark 2. Heat the oil in a large flameproof casserole and add the onion. Cook gently for 10 minutes until soft and lightly browned. Add the garlic and chilli and cook briefly. Increase the heat. Add the chuck steak or lean mince and cook for a further 10 minutes, stirring occasionally, until browned.

Add the chilli powder and stir well. Cook for about 2 minutes, then add the chopped tomatoes and tomato purée. Bring slowly to the boil. Cover and cook in the preheated oven for 1½ hours. Meanwhile, brush a little vegetable oil all over the potatoes and rub on some coarse salt. Put the potatoes in the oven alongside the chilli.

When the 1½ hours are up, remove the chilli from the oven and stir in the kidney beans. Return to the oven for a further 15 minutes.

Remove the chilli and potatoes from the oven. Cut a cross in each potato, then squeeze to open slightly and season to taste with salt and pepper. Serve with the chilli, guacamole and soured cream.

Try this: FOR AN ALTERNATIVE: 172   FOR A POULTRY OR VEGETABLE OPTION: 268

Beef Bourguignon

SERVES 4

675 g/1½ lb braising steak, trimmed	225 g/8 oz carrots, peeled and sliced	salt and freshly ground black pepper
225 g/8 oz piece of pork belly or lardons	2 tbsp plain flour	450 g/1 lb new potatoes, scrubbed
2 tbsp olive oil	3 tbsp brandy (optional)	1 tbsp freshly chopped parsley, to garnish
12 shallots, peeled	150 ml/¼ pint red wine, such as a Burgundy	
2 garlic cloves, peeled and sliced	450 ml/¾ pint beef stock	
	1 bay leaf	

Preheat the oven 160°C/325°F/Gas Mark 3. Cut the steak and pork into small pieces and reserve. Heat 1 tablespoon of the oil in an ovenproof casserole (or frying pan, if preferred), add the meat and cook in batches for 5–8 minutes, or until sealed. Remove with a slotted spoon and reserve.

Add the remaining oil to the casserole/pan, then add the shallots, carrots and garlic and cook for 10 minutes. Return the meat to the casserole/pan and sprinkle in the flour. Cook for 2 minutes, stirring occasionally, before pouring in the brandy. Heat for 1 minute, then take off the heat and ignite.

When the flames have subsided, pour in the wine and stock. Return to the heat and bring to the boil, stirring constantly.

If a frying pan has been used, transfer everything to a casserole, add the bay leaf and season to taste with salt and pepper. Cover with a lid and cook in the oven for 1 hour.

Cut the potatoes in half. Remove the casserole from the oven and add the potatoes. Cook for a further 1 hour, or until the meat and potatoes are tender. Serve sprinkled with chopped parsley.

Try this: FOR AN ALTERNATIVE: 166   FOR A POULTRY OR VEGETABLE OPTION: 202

Poultry

Cheesy Chicken Burgers

SERVES 4

1 tbsp sunflower oil
1 small onion, peeled and
    finely chopped
1 garlic clove, peeled
    and crushed
½ red pepper, deseeded and
    finely chopped
450 g/1 lb fresh chicken mince
2 tbsp 0%-fat Greek yogurt
50 g/2 oz fresh
    brown breadcrumbs

1 tbsp freshly chopped
    herbs, such as parsley or
    tarragon
50 g/2 oz Cheshire
    cheese, crumbled
salt and freshly ground
    black pepper

**For the sweetcorn and
    tomato relish:**
200 g can sweetcorn, drained

1 carrot, peeled, grated
½ green chilli, deseeded
    and finely chopped
2 tsp cider vinegar
2 tsp light soft brown sugar

To serve:
wholemeal or granary rolls
lettuce
sliced tomatoes
mixed salad leaves

Preheat the grill. Heat the oil in a frying pan and gently cook the onion and garlic for 5 minutes. Add the red pepper and cook for 5 minutes. Transfer into a mixing bowl and reserve.

Add the chicken, yogurt, breadcrumbs, herbs and cheese and season to taste with salt and pepper. Mix well. Divide the mixture equally into 6 and shape into burgers. Cover and chill in the refrigerator for at least 20 minutes.

To make the relish, put all the ingredients in a small saucepan with 1 tablespoon of water and heat gently, stirring occasionally until all the sugar has dissolved. Cover and cook over a low heat for 2 minutes, then uncover and cook for a further minute, or until the relish is thick.

Place the burgers on a lightly oiled grill pan and grill under a medium heat for 8–10 minutes on each side, or until browned and completely cooked through.

Warm the rolls if liked, then split in half and fill with the burgers, lettuce, sliced tomatoes and the prepared relish. Serve immediately with the salad leaves.

Try this: FOR AN ALTERNATIVE: 218   FOR A VEGETABLE OPTION: 276

Chicken & Summer Vegetable Risotto

SERVES 4

1 litre/1¾ pint chicken or
   vegetable stock
225 g/8 oz baby
   asparagus spears
125 g/4 oz French beans
15 g/½ oz butter
1 small onion, peeled
and finely chopped
150 ml/¼ pint dry white wine
275 g/10 oz arborio rice
pinch of saffron strands
75 g/3 oz frozen peas,
   thawed
225 g/8 oz cooked chicken,
skinned and diced
juice of ½ lemon
salt and freshly ground
   black pepper
25 g/1 oz Parmesan, shaved

Bring the stock to the boil in a large saucepan. Trim the asparagus and cut into 4 cm/1½ inch lengths. Blanch the asparagus in the stock for 1–2 minutes or until tender, then remove with a slotted spoon and reserve. Halve the green beans and cook in the boiling stock for 4 minutes. Remove and reserve. Turn down the heat and keep the stock barely simmering.

Melt the butter in a heavy-based saucepan. Add the onion and cook gently for about 5 minutes. Pour the wine into the pan and boil rapidly until the liquid has almost reduced. Add the rice and cook, stirring for 1 minute until the grains are coated and look translucent.

Add the saffron and a ladle of the stock. Simmer, stirring all the time, until the stock has absorbed. Continue adding the stock, a ladle at a time, until it has all been absorbed. After 15 minutes the risotto should be creamy with a slight bite to it. If not add a little more stock and cook for a few more minutes, or until it is of the correct texture and consistency. Add the peas, reserved vegetables, chicken and lemon juice. Season to taste with salt and pepper and cook for 3-4 minutes or until the chicken is thoroughly heated and piping hot.

Spoon the risotto on to warmed serving plates. Scatter each portion with a few shavings of Parmesan cheese and serve immediately.

Try this: FOR AN ALTERNATIVE: 196   FOR A VEGETABLE OPTION: 254

Chicken & White Wine Risotto

SERVES 4–6

2 tbsp oil
125 g/4 oz unsalted butter
2 shallots, peeled and
   finely chopped
300 g/11 oz Arborio rice
600 ml/1 pint dry white wine

750 ml/1¼ pints chicken
   stock, heated
350 g/12 oz skinless chicken
   breast fillets, thinly sliced
50 g/2 oz Parmesan cheese,
   grated

2 tbsp freshly chopped dill
   or parsley
salt and freshly ground
   black pepper

Heat the oil and half the butter in a large heavy-based saucepan over a medium-high heat. Add the shallots and cook for 2 minutes, or until softened, stirring frequently. Add the rice and cook for 2–3 minutes, stirring frequently, until the rice is translucent and well coated.

Pour in half the wine; it will bubble and steam rapidly. Cook, stirring constantly, until the liquid is absorbed. Add a ladleful of the hot stock and cook until the liquid is absorbed. Carefully stir in the chicken.

Continue adding the stock, about half a ladleful at a time, allowing each addition to be absorbed before adding the next; never allow the rice to cook dry. This process should take about 20 minutes. The risotto should have a creamy consistency and the rice should be tender, but firm to the bite.

Stir in the remaining wine and cook for 2–3 minutes. Remove from the heat and stir in the remaining butter with the Parmesan cheese and half the chopped herbs. Season to taste with salt and pepper. Spoon into warmed shallow bowls and sprinkle each with the remaining chopped herbs. Serve immediately.

Try this: FOR AN ALTERNATIVE: 194   FOR A VEGETABLE OPTION: 282

Creamy Chicken & Rice Pilau

SERVES 6–8

350 g/12 oz basmati rice
salt and freshly ground
    black pepper
50 g/2 oz butter
100 g/3½ oz flaked almonds
75 g/3 oz unsalted shelled
    pistachio nuts
4–6 skinless chicken
    breast fillets, each cut
    into 4 pieces

2 tbsp vegetable oil
2 medium onions, peeled
    and thinly sliced
2 garlic cloves, peeled and
    finely chopped
2.5 cm/1 inch piece of fresh
    root ginger, finely chopped
6 green cardamom pods,
    lightly crushed
4–6 whole cloves

1 tsp ground coriander
½ tsp cayenne pepper, or
    to taste
2 bay leaves
225 ml/8 fl oz natural yogurt
225 ml/8 fl oz double cream
225 g/8 oz seedless green
    grapes, halved if large
2 tbsp freshly chopped
    coriander or mint

Bring a saucepan of lightly salted water to the boil. Gradually pour in the rice; return to the boil, then simmer for about 12 minutes until tender. Drain, rinse under cold water and reserve.

Heat the butter in a large deep frying pan over a medium-high heat. Add the almonds and pistachios and cook for about 2 minutes, stirring constantly, until golden. Using a slotted spoon, transfer to a plate.

Add the chicken pieces to the pan and cook for 5 minutes, or until golden, turning once. Remove from the pan and reserve. Add the oil to the pan and cook the onions for 10 minutes, or until golden, stirring frequently. Stir in the garlic, ginger, spices and bay leaves and cook for 2–3 minutes, stirring. Add 2–3 tablespoons of the yogurt and cook, stirring until the moisture evaporates. Continue adding the yogurt in this way until it is used up.

Return the chicken and nuts to the pan and stir. Stir in 125 ml/4 fl oz of boiling water and season to taste with salt and pepper. Cook, covered, over a low heat for 10 minutes until the chicken is tender. Stir in the cream, grapes and half the herbs. Gently fold in the rice. Heat through for 5 minutes and sprinkle with the remaining herbs, then serve.

Try this: FOR AN ALTERNATIVE: 196   FOR A VEGETABLE OPTION: 266

Chicken & Ham Pie

SERVES 6

300 g/10½ oz ready-made shortcrust pastry
1 tbsp olive oil
1 leek, trimmed and sliced
175 g/6 oz piece of bacon, cut into small dice
225 g/8 oz cooked boneless chicken meat
2 avocados, peeled, pitted and chopped
1 tbsp lemon juice
salt and freshly ground black pepper
2 large eggs, beaten
150 ml/¼ pint natural yogurt
4 tbsp chicken stock
1 tbsp poppy seeds

To serve:
sliced red onion
mixed salad leaves

Preheat the oven to 200˚C/400˚F/Gas Mark 6. Heat the oil in a frying pan and fry the leek and bacon for 4 minutes until soft but not coloured. Transfer to a bowl and reserve.

Cut the chicken into bite-sized pieces and add to the leek and bacon. Toss the avocado in the lemon juice, add to the chicken and season to taste with salt and pepper.

Roll out half the pastry on a lightly floured surface and use to line a 18 cm/7 inch loose-bottomed deep flan tin.

Mix together 1 egg, the yogurt and the chicken stock. Mix the yogurt mixture with the chicken. Pour the chicken mixture into the pastry case.

Roll out the remaining pastry on a lightly floured surface, and cut out the lid to 5 mm/¼ inch wider than the dish. Brush the rim with the remaining beaten egg and lay the pastry lid on top, pressing to seal. Knock the edges with the back of a knife to seal further. Cut a slit in the lid and brush with the egg.

Sprinkle with the poppy seeds and bake in the preheated oven for about 30 minutes, or until the pastry is golden brown. Serve with the onion and mixed salad leaves.

 Try this: FOR AN ALTERNATIVE: 202 FOR A VEGETABLE OPTION: 292

Sauvignon Chicken & Mushroom Filo Pie

SERVES 4

1 onion, peeled and
chopped
1 leek, trimmed and
chopped
225 ml/8 fl oz chicken stock
3 x 175 g/6 oz chicken
breasts
150 ml/¼ pint dry white wine
1 bay leaf

175 g/6 oz baby
button mushrooms
2 tbsp plain flour
1 tbsp freshly
chopped tarragon
salt and freshly ground
black pepper
sprig of fresh parsley,
to garnish

seasonal vegetables,
to serve

For the topping:
75 g/3 oz (about 5 sheets)
filo pastry
1 tbsp sunflower oil
1 tsp sesame seeds

Preheat the oven to 190°C/375°F/Gas Mark 5. Put the onion and leek in a heavy-based saucepan with 125 ml/4 fl oz of the stock. Bring to the boil, cover and simmer for 5 minutes, then uncover and cook until all the stock has evaporated and the vegetables are tender.

Cut the chicken into bite-sized cubes. Add to the pan with the remaining stock, wine and bay leaf. Cover and gently simmer for 5 minutes. Add the mushrooms and simmer for a further 5 minutes.

Blend the flour with 3 tablespoons of cold water. Stir into the pan and cook, stirring all the time until the sauce has thickened. Stir the tarragon into the sauce and season with salt and pepper.

Spoon the mixture into a 1.2 litre/2 pint pie dish, discarding the bay leaf.

Lightly brush a sheet of filo pastry with a little of the oil. Crumple the pastry slightly. Arrange on top of the filling. Repeat with the remaining filo sheets and oil, then sprinkle the top of the pie with the sesame seeds.

Bake the pie on the middle shelf of the preheated oven for 20 minutes until the filo pastry is golden and crisp. Garnish with a sprig of parsley. Serve immediately with the seasonal vegetables.

Try this: FOR AN ALTERNATIVE: 200   FOR A VEGETABLE OPTION: 294

Chicken Pie with Sweet Potato Topping

SERVES 4

250 g/9 oz potatoes, peeled and cut into chunks
700 g/1½ lb sweet potatoes, peeled and cut into chunks
150 ml/¼ pint milk
25 g/1 oz butter
2 tsp brown sugar
grated rind of 1 orange

salt and freshly ground black pepper
4 skinless chicken breast fillets, diced
1 medium onion, peeled and coarsely chopped
125 g/4 oz baby mushrooms, stems trimmed
2 leeks, trimmed and

thickly sliced
150 ml/¼ pint dry white wine
1 chicken stock cube
1 tbsp freshly chopped parsley
50 ml/2 fl oz crème fraîche or thick double cream
green vegetables, to serve

Preheat the oven to 190°C/375°F/Gas Mark 5, 10 minutes before required. Cook the potatoes and sweet potatoes in lightly salted boiling water until tender. Drain well, then return to the saucepan and mash until smooth and creamy, gradually adding the milk, then the butter, sugar and orange rind. Season to taste with salt and pepper and reserve.

Place the chicken in a saucepan with the onion, mushrooms, leeks, wine, stock cube and season to taste. Simmer, covered, until the chicken and vegetables are tender. Using a slotted spoon, transfer the chicken and vegetables to a 1.1 litre/2 pint pie dish. Add the parsley and crème fraîche or cream to the liquid in the pan and bring to the boil. Simmer until thickened and smooth, stirring constantly. Pour over the chicken in the pie dish, mix and cool.

Spread the mashed potato over the chicken filling, and swirl the surface into decorative peaks. Bake in the preheated oven for 35 minutes, or until the top is golden and the chicken filling is heated through. Serve immediately with fresh green vegetables.

Try this: FOR AN ALTERNATIVE: 202   FOR A VEGETABLE OPTION: 258

Chicken & New Potatoes on Rosemary Skewers

SERVES 4

8 thick fresh rosemary stems, at least 23 cm/ 9 inches long
3–4 tbsp extra-virgin olive oil
2 garlic cloves, peeled and crushed
1 tsp freshly chopped thyme

grated rind and juice of 1 lemon
salt and freshly ground black pepper
4 skinless chicken breast fillets
16 small new potatoes, peeled or scrubbed

8 very small onions or shallots, peeled
1 large yellow or red pepper, deseeded
lemon wedges, to garnish
parsley-flavoured cooked rice, to serve

Preheat the grill and line the grill rack with tinfoil just before cooking. If using a barbecue, light at least 20 minutes before required. Strip the leaves from the rosemary stems, leaving about 5 cm/2 inches of soft leaves at the top. Chop the leaves coarsely and reserve. Using a sharp knife, cut the thicker woody ends of the stems to a point which can pierce the chicken pieces and potatoes. Blend the chopped rosemary, oil, garlic, thyme and lemon rind and juice in a shallow dish. Season to taste with salt and pepper. Cut the chicken into 4 cm/½ inch cubes, add to the flavoured oil and stir well. Cover, refrigerate for at least 30 minutes, turning occasionally.

Cook the potatoes in lightly salted boiling water for 10–12 minutes until just tender. Add the onions to the potatoes 2 minutes before the end of the cooking time. Drain, rinse under cold running water and leave to cool. Cut the pepper into 2.5 cm/1 inch squares.

Beginning with a piece of chicken and starting with the pointed end of the skewer, alternately thread equal amounts of chicken, potato, pepper and onion onto each rosemary skewer. Cover the leafy ends of the skewers with tinfoil to stop them from burning. Do not thread the chicken and vegetables too closely together on the skewer or the chicken may not cook completely. Cook the kebabs for 15 minutes, or until tender and golden, turning and brushing with either extra oil or the marinade. Remove the tinfoil, garnish with lemon wedges and serve on rice.

Try this: FOR AN ALTERNATIVE: 208   FOR A VEGETABLE OPTION: 268

Slow Roast Chicken with Potatoes & Oregano

SERVES 6

1.4–1.8 kg/3–4 lb oven-ready chicken, preferably free range
1 lemon, halved
1 onion, peeled and quartered

50 g/2 oz butter, softened
salt and freshly ground black pepper
1 kg/2¼ lb potatoes, peeled and quartered
3–4 tbsp extra-virgin olive oil

1 tbsp dried oregano, crumbled
1 tsp fresh thyme leaves
2 tbsp freshly chopped thyme

Preheat the oven to 200˚C/400˚F/Gas Mark 6. Rinse the chicken and dry well, inside and out, with absorbent kitchen paper. Rub the chicken all over with the lemon halves, then squeeze the juice over it and into the cavity. Put the squeezed halves into the cavity with the quartered onion. Rub the softened butter all over the chicken and season to taste with salt and pepper, then put it in a large roasting tin, breast-side down.

Toss the potatoes in the oil, season with salt and pepper to taste and add the dried oregano and fresh thyme. Arrange the potatoes with the oil around the chicken and carefully pour 150 ml/¼ pint water into one end of the pan (not over the oil). Roast in the preheated oven for 25 minutes. Reduce the oven temperature to 190˚C/375˚F/Gas Mark 5 and turn the chicken breast-side up. Turn the potatoes, sprinkle over half the fresh herbs and baste the chicken and potatoes with the juices. Continue roasting for 1 hour, or until the chicken is cooked, basting occasionally. If the liquid evaporates completely, add a little more water. The chicken is done when the juices run clear when the thigh is pierced with a skewer. Transfer the chicken to a carving board and rest for 5 minutes, covered with tinfoil. Return the potatoes to the oven while the chicken is resting.

Carve the chicken into pieces and arrange on a large heatproof serving dish with the potatoes around it and drizzle over any remaining juices. Sprinkle with the remaining herbs and serve.

Try this: FOR AN ALTERNATIVE: 206 FOR A VEGETABLE OPTION: 270

Orange–roasted Whole Chicken

SERVES 6

1 small orange, thinly sliced
50 g/2 oz sugar
1.4 kg/3 lb oven-ready chicken
1 small bunch fresh coriander
1 small bunch fresh mint
2 tbsp olive oil

1 tsp Chinese five-
    spice powder
½ tsp paprika
1 tsp fennel seeds, crushed
salt and freshly ground
    black pepper

sprigs of fresh coriander,
    to garnish
freshly cooked vegetables,
    to serve

Preheat the oven to 190°C/375°F/Gas Mark 5, 10 minutes before cooking. Place the orange slices in a small saucepan, cover with water, bring to the boil, then simmer for 2 minutes and drain. Place the sugar in a clean saucepan with 150 ml/¼ pint fresh water. Stir over a low heat until the sugar dissolves, then bring to the boil, add the drained orange slices and simmer for 10 minutes. Remove from the heat and leave in the syrup until cold.

Remove any excess fat from inside the chicken. Starting at the neck end, carefully loosen the skin of the chicken over the breast and legs without tearing. Push the orange slices under the loosened skin with the coriander and mint.

Mix together the olive oil, Chinese five-spice powder, paprika and crushed fennel seeds and season to taste with salt and pepper. Brush the chicken skin generously with this mixture. Transfer to a wire rack set over a roasting tin and roast in the preheated oven for 1½ hours, or until the juices run clear when a skewer is inserted into the thickest part of the thigh. Remove from the oven and leave to rest for 10 minutes. Garnish with sprigs of fresh coriander and serve with freshly cooked vegetables.

 Try this: FOR AN ALTERNATIVE: 212   FOR A VEGETABLE OPTION: 288

Herbed Hasselback Potatoes with Roast Chicken

SERVES 4

8 medium, evenly-sized
   potatoes, peeled
3 large sprigs of
   fresh rosemary
1 tbsp oil
salt and freshly ground

black pepper
350 g/12 oz baby
   parsnips, peeled
350 g/12 oz baby
   carrots, peeled
350 g/12 oz baby

leeks, trimmed
75 g/3 oz butter
finely grated rind of
   1 lemon, preferably
   unwaxed
1.6 kg/3½ lb chicken

Preheat the oven to 200°C/400°F/Gas Mark 6, about 15 minutes before cooking. Place a chopstick on either side of a potato and, with a sharp knife, cut down through the potato until you reach the chopsticks; take care not to cut right through the potato. Repeat these cuts every 5 mm/¼ inch along the length of the potato. Carefully ease 2–4 of the slices apart and slip in a few rosemary sprigs. Repeat with remaining potatoes. Brush with the oil and season well with salt and pepper.

Place the seasoned potatoes in a large roasting tin. Add the parsnips, carrots and leeks to the potatoes in the tin, cover with a wire rack or trivet.

Beat the butter and lemon rind together and season to taste. Smear the chicken with the lemon butter and place on the rack over the vegetables.

Roast in the preheated oven for 1 hour 40 minutes, basting the chicken and vegetables occasionally, until cooked thoroughly. The juices should run clear when the thigh is pierced with a skewer. Place the cooked chicken on a warmed serving platter, arrange the roast vegetables around it and serve immediately.

 Try this: FOR AN ALTERNATIVE: 210   FOR A VEGETABLE OPTION: 256

Braised Chicken in Beer

SERVES 4

4 chicken joints, skinned
125 g/4 oz pitted dried prunes
2 bay leaves
12 shallots
2 tsp olive oil
125 g/4 oz small button
　　mushrooms, wiped
1 tsp soft dark brown sugar

½ tsp wholegrain mustard
2 tsp tomato purée
150 ml/¼ pint light ale
150 ml/¼ pint chicken stock
salt and freshly ground
　　black pepper
2 tsp cornflour
2 tsp lemon juice

2 tbsp fresh parsley,
　　chopped
flat-leaf parsley, to garnish

To serve:
mashed potatoes
seasonal green vegetables

Preheat the oven to 170°C/325°F/Gas Mark 3. Cut each chicken joint in half and put in an ovenproof casserole with the prunes and bay leaves.

To peel the shallots, put in a small bowl and cover with boiling water. Drain them after 2 minutes and rinse under cold water until cool enough to handle. The skins should then peel away easily.

Heat the oil in a large non-stick frying pan. Add the shallots and gently cook for about 5 minutes until beginning to colour. Add the mushrooms to the pan and cook for a further 3–4 minutes until both the mushrooms and onions are softened. Sprinkle the sugar over the shallots and mushrooms, then add the mustard, tomato purée, ale and chicken stock. Season to taste with salt and pepper and bring to the boil, stirring to combine. Carefully pour over the chicken.

Cover the casserole and cook in the preheated oven for 1 hour. Blend the cornflour with the lemon juice and 1 tablespoon of cold water and stir into the chicken casserole. Return the casserole to the oven for a further 10 minutes or until the chicken is cooked and the vegetables are tender.

Remove the bay leaves and stir in the chopped parsley. Garnish the chicken with the flat-leaf parsley. Serve with the mashed potatoes and fresh green vegetables.

Try this: FOR AN ALTERNATIVE: 202　FOR A VEGETABLE OPTION: 262

Chicken Baked in a Salt Crust

SERVES 4

1.8 kg/4 lb oven-ready chicken
salt and freshly ground
　　black pepper
1 medium onion, peeled
sprig of fresh rosemary
sprig of fresh thyme
1 bay leaf
15 g/½ oz butter, softened

1 garlic clove, peeled
　　and crushed
pinch of ground paprika
finely grated rind of ½ lemon

To garnish:
fresh herbs
lemon slices

**For the salt crust (to be
　　discarded after cooking):**
900 g/2 lb plain flour
450 g/1 lb fine cooking salt
450 g/1 lb coarse sea salt
2 tbsp oil

Preheat the oven to 170°C/325°F/Gas Mark 3. Remove the giblets if necessary and rinse the chicken with cold water. Sprinkle the inside with salt and pepper. Put the onion inside with the rosemary, thyme and bay leaf.

Mix the butter, garlic, paprika and lemon rind together. Starting at the neck end, gently ease the skin from the chicken and push the mixture under.

To make the salt crust, put the flour and salts in a large mixing bowl and stir together. Make a well in the centre. Pour in 600 ml/1 pint of cold water and the oil. Mix to a stiff dough, then knead on a lightly floured surface for 2–3 minutes. Roll out the pastry to a circle with a diameter of about 51 cm/20 inches. Place the chicken breast side down in the middle. Lightly brush the edges with water, then fold over to enclose. Pinch the joints together to seal.

Put the chicken join side down in a roasting tin and cook in the preheated oven for 2¾ hours. Remove from the oven and stand for 20 minutes.

Break open the hard crust and remove the chicken. Discard the crust. Remove the skin from the chicken, garnish with the fresh herbs and lemon slices. Serve the chicken immediately.

Try this: FOR AN ALTERNATIVE: 208　FOR A VEGETABLE OPTION: 290

Cheesy Baked Chicken Macaroni

SERVES 4

1 tbsp olive oil
350 g/12 oz boneless
    and skinless chicken
    breasts, diced
75 g/3 oz pancetta,
    diced
1 onion, peeled
    and chopped

1 garlic clove, peeled
    and chopped
350 g packet fresh
    tomato sauce
400 g can chopped tomatoes
2 tbsp freshly chopped basil,
    plus leaves to garnish
salt and freshly ground

black pepper
350 g/12 oz macaroni
150 g/5oz mozzarella cheese,
    drained and chopped
50 g/2 oz Gruyère
    cheese, grated
50 g/2 oz freshly grated
    Parmesan cheese

Preheat the grill just before cooking. Heat the oil in large frying pan and cook the chicken for 8 minutes, or until browned, stirring occasionally. Drain on absorbent kitchen paper and reserve. Add the pancetta slices to the pan and fry on both sides until crispy. Remove from the pan and reserve.

Add the onion and garlic to the frying pan and cook for 5 minutes, or until softened. Stir in the tomato sauce, chopped tomatoes and basil and season to taste with salt and pepper. Bring to the boil, lower the heat and simmer the sauce for 5 minutes.

Meanwhile, bring a large pan of lightly salted water to a rolling boil. Add the macaroni and cook according to the packet instructions, or until 'al dente'.

Drain the macaroni thoroughly, return to the pan and stir in the sauce, chicken and mozzarella cheese. Spoon into a shallow ovenproof dish.

Sprinkle the pancetta over the macaroni. Sprinkle over the Gruyère and Parmesan cheeses. Place under the preheated grill and cook for 5–10 minutes, or until golden-brown; turn the dish occasionally. Garnish and serve immediately.

Try this: FOR AN ALTERNATIVE: 192   FOR A VEGETABLE OPTION: 280

Chicken Tagliatelle

SERVES 4

350 g/12 oz tagliatelle
125 g/4 oz frozen peas
4 boneless and skinless
   chicken breasts
2 tbsp olive oil
¼ cucumber, cut into strips

150 ml/¼ pint dry vermouth
150 ml/¼ pint double cream
125 g/4 oz Stilton cheese,
   crumbled
3 tbsp freshly snipped
   chives, plus extra

   to garnish
salt and freshly ground
   black pepper
fresh herbs, to garnish

Bring a large pan of lightly salted water to a rolling boil. Add the pasta and cook according to the packet instructions, or until 'al dente'. Add the peas to the pan 5 minutes before the end of cooking time and cook until tender. Drain the pasta and peas, return to the pan and keep warm.

Trim the chicken if necessary, then cut into bite-sized pieces. Heat the olive oil in a large frying pan, add the chicken and cook for 8 minutes, or until golden, stirring occasionally.

Add the cucumber and cook for 2 minutes, or until slightly softened, stirring occasionally. Stir in the vermouth, bring to the boil, then lower the heat and simmer for 3 minutes, or until reduced slightly.

Add the cream to the pan, bring to the boil, stirring constantly, then stir in the Stilton cheese and snipped chives. Season to taste with salt and pepper. Heat through thoroughly, stirring occasionally, until the cheese is just beginning to melt.

Toss the chicken mixture into the pasta. Tip into a warmed serving dish or on to individual plates. Garnish and serve immediately.

Try this: FOR AN ALTERNATIVE: 222 FOR A VEGETABLE OPTION: 276

Herb–baked Chicken with Tagliatelle

SERVES 4

75 g/3 oz fresh
   white breadcrumbs
3 tbsp olive oil
1 tsp dried oregano
2 tbsp sun-dried
   tomato paste

salt and freshly ground
   black pepper
4 boneless and skinless
   chicken breasts, each
   about 150 g/5 oz
2 x 400 g cans

   plum tomatoes
4 tbsp freshly chopped basil
2 tbsp dry white wine
350 g/12 oz tagliatelle
fresh basil sprigs,
   to garnish

Preheat the oven to 200°C/400°F/Gas Mark 6, 15 minute before cooking. Mix together the breadcrumbs, 1 tablespoon of the olive oil, the oregano and tomato paste. Season to taste with salt and pepper. Place the chicken breasts well apart in a roasting tin and coat with the breadcrumb mixture.

Mix the plum tomatoes with the chopped basil and white wine. Season to taste, then spoon evenly round the chicken.

Drizzle the remaining olive oil over the chicken breasts and cook in the preheated oven for 20–30 minutes, or until the chicken is golden and the juices run clear when a skewer is inserted into the flesh.

Meanwhile, bring a large pan of lightly salted water to a rolling boil. Add the pasta and cook according to the packet instructions, or until 'al dente'.

Drain the pasta thoroughly and transfer to warmed serving plates. Arrange the chicken breasts on top of the pasta and spoon over the sauce. Garnish with sprigs of basil and serve immediately.

Try this: FOR AN ALTERNATIVE: 220   FOR A VEGETABLE OPTION: 254

Warm Chicken & Potato Salad with Peas & Mint

SERVES 4-6

450 g/1 lb new potatoes, peeled or scrubbed and cut into bite-sized pieces
salt and freshly ground black pepper
2 tbsp cider vinegar
175 g/6 oz frozen garden peas, thawed

1 small ripe avocado
4 cooked chicken breasts, about 450 g/1 lb in weight, skinned and diced
2 tbsp freshly chopped mint
2 heads Little Gem lettuce
fresh mint sprigs, to garnish

For the dressing:
2 tbsp raspberry or sherry vinegar
2 tsp Dijon mustard
1 tsp clear honey
50 ml/2 fl oz sunflower oil
50 ml/2 fl oz extra virgin olive oil

Cook the potatoes in lightly salted boiling water for 15 minutes, or until just tender when pierced with the tip of a sharp knife; do not overcook. Rinse under cold running water to cool slightly, then drain and turn into a large bowl. Sprinkle with the cider vinegar and toss gently.

Run the peas under hot water to ensure that they are thawed, pat dry with absorbent kitchen paper and add to the potatoes.

Cut the avocado in half lengthways and remove the stone. Peel and cut the avocado into cubes and add to the potatoes and peas. Add the chicken and stir together lightly.

To make the dressing, place all the ingredients in a screw-top jar, with a little salt and pepper and shake well to mix; add a little more oil if the flavour is too sharp. Pour over the salad and toss gently to coat. Sprinkle in half the mint and stir lightly.

Separate the lettuce leaves and spread onto a large shallow serving plate. Spoon the salad on top and sprinkle with the remaining mint. Garnish with mint sprigs and serve.

Try this: FOR AN ALTERNATIVE: 236   FOR A VEGETABLE OPTION: 270

Stir–fried Lemon Chicken

SERVES 4

350 g/12 oz boneless,
   skinless chicken breast
1 large egg white
5 tsp cornflour
3 tbsp vegetable or
   groundnut oil
150 ml/¼ pint chicken stock

2 tbsp fresh lemon juice
2 tbsp light soy sauce
1 tbsp Chinese rice wine or
   dry sherry
1 tbsp sugar
2 garlic cloves, peeled and
   finely chopped

¼ tsp dried chilli flakes,
   or to taste

To garnish:
lemon rind strips
red chilli slices

Using a sharp knife, trim the chicken, discarding any fat and cut into thin strips, about 5 cm/2 inch long and 1 cm/½ inch wide. Place in a shallow dish. Lightly whisk the egg white and 1 tablespoon of the cornflour together until smooth. Pour over the chicken strips and mix well until coated evenly. Leave to marinate in the refrigerator for at least 20 minutes.

When ready to cook, drain the chicken and reserve. Heat a wok or large frying pan, add the oil and when hot, add the chicken and stir-fry for 1–2 minutes, or until the chicken has turned white. Using a slotted spoon, remove from the wok and reserve.

Wipe the wok clean and return to the heat. Add the chicken stock, lemon juice, soy sauce, Chinese rice wine or sherry, sugar, garlic and chilli flakes and bring to the boil. Blend the remaining cornflour with 1 tablespoon of water and stir into the stock. Simmer for 1 minute.

Return the chicken to the wok and continue simmering for a further 2–3 minutes, or until the chicken is tender and the sauce has thickened. Garnish with lemon strips and red chilli slices. Serve immediately.

Try this: FOR AN ALTERNATIVE: 242 FOR A VEGETABLE OPTION: 284

Chicken Tikka Masala

SERVES 4

4 skinless chicken
   breast fillets
150 ml/¼ pint natural yogurt
1 garlic clove,
   peeled and crushed
2.5 cm/1 inch piece fresh
   root ginger, peeled
   and grated
1 tsp chilli powder

1 tbsp ground coriander
2 tbsp lime juice
twist of lime, to garnish
freshly cooked rice, to serve

For the masala sauce:
15 g/½ oz unsalted butter
2 tbsp sunflower oil
1 onion, peeled

   and chopped
1 green chilli, deseeded and
   finely chopped
1 tsp garam masala
150 ml/¼ pint double cream
salt and freshly ground
   black pepper
3 tbsp fresh coriander
   leaves, roughly torn

Preheat the oven to 200°C/400°F/Gas Mark 6, 15 minutes before cooking. Cut each chicken breast across into three pieces, then make two or three shallow cuts in each piece. Put in a shallow dish. Mix together the yogurt, garlic, ginger, chilli powder, ground coriander and lime juice. Pour over the chicken, cover and marinate in the refrigerator for up to 24 hours.

Remove the chicken from the marinade and arrange on an oiled baking tray. Bake in the preheated oven for 15 minutes, or until golden brown and cooked.

While the chicken is cooking, heat the butter and oil in a wok and stir-fry the onion for 5 minutes, or until tender. Add the chilli and garam masala and stir-fry for a few more seconds. Stir in the cream and remaining marinade. Simmer over a low heat for 1 minute, stirring all the time.

Add the chicken pieces and cook for a further 1 minute, stirring to coat in the sauce. Season to taste with salt and pepper. Transfer the chicken pieces to a warmed serving plate. Stir the chopped coriander into the sauce, then spoon over the chicken, garnish and serve immediately with freshly cooked rice.

Try this: FOR AN ALTERNATIVE: 238   FOR A VEGETABLE OPTION: 286

Chicken Chow Mein

SERVES 4

225 g/8 oz egg noodles
5 tsp sesame oil
4 tsp light soy sauce
2 tbsp Chinese rice wine or
  dry sherry
salt and freshly ground black
  pepper
225 g/8 oz skinless chicken

breast fillets, cut into
  strips
3 tbsp groundnut oil
2 garlic cloves, peeled and
  finely chopped
50 g/2 oz mangetout peas,
  finely sliced
50 g/2 oz cooked ham, cut

into fine strips
2 tsp dark soy sauce
pinch of sugar

To garnish:
shredded spring onions
toasted sesame seeds

Bring a large saucepan of water to the boil and add the noodles. Cook for 3–5 minutes, drain and plunge into cold water. Drain again, add 1 tablespoon of the sesame oil and stir lightly.

Place 2 teaspoons of light soy sauce, 1 tablespoon of Chinese rice wine or sherry, and 1 teaspoon of the sesame oil, with seasoning to taste in a bowl. Add the chicken and stir well. Cover lightly and leave to marinate in the refrigerator for about 15 minutes.

Heat the wok over a high heat, add 1 tablespoon of the groundnut oil and when very hot, add the chicken and its marinade and stir-fry for 2 minutes. Remove the chicken and juices and reserve. Wipe the wok clean with absorbent kitchen paper.

Reheat the wok and add the oil. Add the garlic and toss in the oil for 20 seconds. Add the mangetout peas and the ham and stir-fry for 1 minute. Add the noodles, remaining light soy sauce, Chinese rice wine or sherry, the dark soy sauce and sugar. Season to taste with salt and pepper and stir-fry for 2 minutes.

Add the chicken and juices to the wok and stir-fry for 4 minutes, or until the chicken is cooked. Drizzle over the remaining sesame oil. Garnish with spring onions and sesame seeds and serve.

   Try this: FOR AN ALTERNATIVE: 234   FOR A VEGETABLE OPTION: 282

Chicken & Baby Vegetable Stir Fry

SERVES 4

2 tbsp groundnut oil
1 small red chilli, deseeded
and finely chopped
150 g/5 oz chicken breast
or thigh meat, skinned
and cut into cubes
2 baby leeks, trimmed
and sliced
12 asparagus spears, halved

125 g/4 oz mangetout peas,
trimmed
125 g/4 oz baby carrots,
trimmed and halved
lengthways
125 g/4 oz fine green beans,
trimmed and diagonally
sliced
125 g/4 oz baby sweetcorn,

diagonally halved
50 ml/2 fl oz chicken stock
2 tsp light soy sauce
1 tbsp dry sherry
1 tsp sesame oil
toasted sesame seeds,
to garnish

Heat the wok until very hot and add the oil. Add the chopped chilli and chicken and stir-fry for 4–5 minutes, or until the chicken is cooked and golden.

Increase the heat, add the leeks to the chicken and stir-fry for 2 minutes. Add the asparagus spears, mangetout peas, baby carrots, green beans, and baby sweetcorn. Stir-fry for 3–4 minutes, or until the vegetables soften slightly but still retain a slight crispness.

In a small bowl, mix together the chicken stock, soy sauce, dry sherry and sesame oil. Pour into the wok, stir and cook until heated through. Sprinkle with the toasted sesame seeds and serve immediately.

Try this: FOR AN ALTERNATIVE: 226   FOR A VEGETABLE OPTION: 284

Deep–fried Chicken Wings

SERVES 4

2 tsp turmeric
1 tsp hot chilli powder
1 tsp ground coriander
1 tsp ground cumin
3 garlic cloves, peeled
   and crushed

8 chicken wings
2 tbsp orange marmalade
2 tbsp ginger preserve
   or marmalade
1 tsp salt
3 tbsp rice wine vinegar

2 tbsp tomato ketchup
1 litre/1¾ pints vegetable oil
   for deep frying
lime wedges, to garnish

Blend the turmeric, chilli powder, ground coriander, ground cumin and garlic together in a small bowl. Dry the chicken wings thoroughly, using absorbent kitchen paper, then rub the spice mixture on to the skin of each chicken wing. Cover and chill in the refrigerator for at least 2 hours.

Meanwhile, make the dipping sauce by mixing together the marmalade, ginger preserve, salt, rice wine vinegar and tomato ketchup in a small saucepan. Heat until blended, leave to cool, then serve. If using straight away, spoon into a small dipping bowl, but if using later, pour into a container with a close-fitting lid and store in the refrigerator.

Pour the oil into the wok and heat to 190˚C/375˚F, or until a small cube of bread dropped in the oil turns golden brown in 30 seconds. Cook 2–3 chicken wings at a time, lowering them into the hot oil, and frying for 3–4 minutes. Remove the wings using a slotted spoon, and drain on absorbent kitchen paper. You may need to reheat the oil before cooking each batch.

When all the chicken wings are cooked, arrange on a warmed serving dish, garnish with the lime wedges and serve.

Try this: FOR AN ALTERNATIVE: 230   FOR A VEGETABLE OPTION: 264

Turkey Hash with Potato & Beetroot

SERVES 4–6

2 tbsp vegetable oil
50 g/2 oz butter
4 slices streaky bacon, diced or sliced
1 medium onion, peeled and finely chopped

450 g/1 lb cooked turkey, diced
450 g/1 lb finely chopped cooked potatoes
2–3 tbsp freshly chopped parsley

2 tbsp plain flour
250 g/9 oz cooked medium beetroot, diced
green salad, to serve

In a large, heavy-based frying pan, heat the oil and half the butter over a medium heat until sizzling. Add the bacon and cook for 4 minutes, or until crisp and golden, stirring occasionally. Using a slotted spoon, transfer to a large bowl. Add the onion to the pan and cook for 3–4 minutes, or until soft and golden, stirring frequently.

Meanwhile, add the turkey, potatoes, parsley and flour to the cooked bacon in the bowl. Stir and toss gently, then fold in the diced beetroot.

Add half the remaining butter to the frying pan and then the turkey vegetable mixture. Stir, then spread the mixture to evenly cover the bottom of the frying pan. Cook for 15 minutes, or until the underside is crisp and brown, pressing the hash firmly into a cake with a spatula. Remove from the heat.

Invert a large plate over the frying pan and, holding the plate and frying pan together with an oven glove, turn the hash out onto the plate. Heat the remaining butter in the pan, slide the hash back into the pan and cook for 4 minutes, or until crisp and brown on the other side. Invert onto the plate again and serve immediately with a green salad.

Try this: FOR AN ALTERNATIVE: 242   FOR A VEGETABLE OPTION: 296

Creamy Turkey & Tomato Pasta

SERVES 4

4 tbsp olive oil
450 g/1 lb turkey breasts,
   cut into bite-sized pieces
550 g/1¼ lb cherry tomatoes,
   on the vine

2 garlic cloves, peeled
   and chopped
4 tbsp balsamic vinegar
4 tbsp freshly chopped basil
salt and freshly ground

   black pepper
200 ml tub crème fraîche
350 g/12 oz tagliatelle
shaved Parmesan cheese,
   to garnish

Preheat the oven to 200°C/400°F/Gas Mark 6. Heat 2 tablespoons of the olive oil in a large frying pan. Add the turkey and cook for 5 minutes, or until sealed, turning occasionally. Transfer to a roasting tin and add the remaining olive oil, the vine tomatoes, garlic and balsamic vinegar. Stir well and season to taste with salt and pepper. Cook in the preheated oven for 30 minutes, or until the turkey is tender, turning the tomatoes and turkey once.

Meanwhile, bring a large pan of lightly salted water to a rolling boil. Add the pasta and cook according to the packet instructions, or until 'al dente'. Drain, return to the pan and keep warm. Stir the basil and seasoning into the crème fraîche.

Remove the roasting tin from the oven and discard the vines. Stir the crème fraîche and basil mix into the turkey and tomato mixture and return to the oven for 1–2 minutes, or until thoroughly heated through.

Stir the turkey and tomato mixture into the pasta and toss lightly together. Tip into a warmed serving dish. Garnish with Parmesan cheese shavings and serve immediately.

 Try this: FOR AN ALTERNATIVE: 198   FOR A VEGETABLE OPTION: 274

Turkey & Mixed Mushroom Lasagne

SERVES 4

1 tbsp olive oil
225 g/8 oz mixed
 mushrooms e.g. button,
 chestnut and portabello,
 wiped and sliced
15 g/½ oz butter
25 g/1 oz plain flour
300 ml/½ pint skimmed milk
1 bay leaf
225 g/8 oz cooked

turkey, cubed
¼ tsp freshly grated nutmeg
salt and freshly ground
 black pepper
400 g can plum tomatoes,
 drained and chopped
1 tsp dried mixed herbs
9 lasagne sheets (about
 150 g/5 oz)

For the topping:
200 ml/7 fl oz 0%-fat
 Greek yogurt
1 medium egg,
 lightly beaten
1 tbsp finely grated
 Parmesan cheese
mixed salad leaves,
 to serve

Preheat the oven to 180°C/350°F/Gas 4. Heat the oil and cook the mushrooms until tender and all the juices have evaporated. Remove and reserve.

Put the butter, flour, milk and bay leaf in the pan. Slowly bring to the boil, stirring until thickened. Simmer for 2–3 minutes. Remove the bay leaf and stir in the mushrooms, turkey, nutmeg, salt and pepper.

Mix together the tomatoes, mixed herbs and season with salt and pepper. Spoon half into the base of a 1.7 litre/3 pint ovenproof dish. Top with 3 sheets of lasagne, then with half the turkey mixture. Repeat the layers, then arrange the remaining 3 sheets of pasta on top.

Mix together the yogurt and egg. Spoon over the lasagne, spreading the mixture into the corners. Sprinkle with the Parmesan and bake in the preheated oven for 45 minutes. Serve with the mixed salad.

Try this: FOR AN ALTERNATIVE: 222 FOR A VEGETABLE OPTION: 278

Turkey & Vegetable Stir Fry

SERVES 4

350 g/12 oz mixed
 vegetables, such as baby
 sweetcorn, 1 small red
 pepper, pak choi,
 mushrooms, broccoli
 florets and baby carrots
1 red chilli
2 tbsp groundnut oil
350 g/12 oz skinless,
 boneless turkey breast,
 sliced into fine strips
 across the grain

2 garlic cloves, peeled and
 finely chopped
2.5 cm/1 inch piece fresh
 root ginger, peeled and
 finely grated
3 spring onions, trimmed
 and finely sliced
2 tbsp light soy sauce
1 tbsp Chinese rice wine
 or dry sherry
2 tbsp chicken stock or water
1 tsp cornflour

1 tsp sesame oil
freshly cooked noodles
 or rice, to serve

To garnish:
50 g/2 oz toasted
 cashew nuts
2 spring onions,
 finely shredded
25 g/1 oz beansprouts

Slice or chop the vegetables into small pieces, depending on which you use. Halve the baby sweetcorn lengthways, deseed and thinly slice the red pepper, tear or shred the pak choi, slice the mushrooms, break the broccoli into small florets and cut the carrots into matchsticks. Deseed and finely chop the chilli.

Heat a wok or large frying pan, add the oil and when hot, add the turkey strips and stir-fry for 1 minute or until they turn white. Add the garlic, ginger, spring onions and chilli and cook for a few seconds. Add the prepared carrot, pepper, broccoli and mushrooms and stir-fry for 1 minute. Add the baby sweetcorn and pak choi and stir-fry for 1 minute.

Blend the soy sauce, Chinese rice wine or sherry and stock or water and pour over the vegetables. Blend the cornflour with 1 teaspoon of water and stir into the vegetables, mixing well. Bring to the boil, reduce the heat, then simmer for 1 minute. Stir in the sesame oil. Tip into a warmed serving dish, sprinkle with cashew nuts, shredded spring onions and beansprouts. Serve immediately with noodles or rice.

Try this: FOR AN ALTERNATIVE: 232   FOR A VEGETABLE OPTION: 284

Duck with Berry Sauce

SERVES 4

4 x 175 g/6 oz boneless
   duck breasts
salt and freshly ground
   black pepper
1 tsp sunflower oil

For the sauce:
juice of 1 orange

1 bay leaf
3 tbsp redcurrant jelly
150 g/5 oz fresh or frozen
   mixed berries
2 tbsp dried cranberries
   or cherries
½ tsp soft light brown sugar
1 tbsp balsamic vinegar

1 tsp freshly chopped mint
sprigs of fresh mint,
   to garnish

To serve:
freshly cooked potatoes
freshly cooked green beans

Remove the skins from the duck breasts and season with a little salt and pepper. Brush a griddle pan with the oil, then heat on the stove until smoking hot.

Place the duck, skinned-side down in the pan. Cook over a medium-high heat for 5 minutes, or until well browned. Turn the duck and cook for 2 minutes. Lower the heat and cook for a further 5–8 minutes, or until cooked, but still slightly pink in the centre. Remove from the pan and keep warm.

While the duck is cooking, make the sauce. Put the orange juice, bay leaf, redcurrant jelly, fresh or frozen and dried berries and sugar in a small griddle pan. Add any juices left in the griddle pan to the small pan. Slowly bring to the boil, lower the heat and simmer uncovered for 4–5 minutes, until the fruit is soft.

Remove the bay leaf. Stir in the vinegar and chopped mint and season to taste with salt and pepper.

Slice the duck breasts on the diagonal and arrange on serving plates. Spoon over the berry sauce and garnish with sprigs of fresh mint. Serve immediately with the potatoes and green beans.

 Try this: FOR AN ALTERNATIVE: 210   FOR A VEGETABLE OPTION: 262

Sticky–glazed Spatchcocked Poussins

SERVES 4

2 poussins, each about
   700 g/1½ lb
salt and freshly ground
   black pepper
4 kumquats, thinly sliced
assorted salad leaves,
   crusty bread or new

potatoes, to serve

For the glaze:
zest of 1 small lemon,
   finely grated
1 tbsp lemon juice
1 tbsp dry sherry

2 tbsp clear honey
2 tbsp dark soy sauce
2 tbsp whole-grain mustard
1 tsp tomato purée
½ tsp Chinese five-
   spice powder

Preheat the grill just before cooking. Place one of the poussins breast-side down on a board. Using poultry shears, cut down one side of the backbone. Cut down the other side of the backbone. Remove the bone. Open out the poussin and press down hard on the breast bone with the heel of your hand to break it and to flatten the poussin.

Thread two skewers crosswise through the bird to keep it flat, ensuring that each skewer goes through a wing and out through the leg on the opposite side. Repeat with the other bird. Season both sides of the bird with salt and pepper.

To make the glaze, mix together the lemon zest and juice, sherry, honey, soy sauce, mustard, tomato purée and Chinese five-spice powder and use to brush all over the poussins.

Place the poussins skin-side down on a grill rack and grill under a medium heat for 15 minutes, brushing halfway through with more glaze. Turn the poussins over and grill for 10 minutes. Brush again with glaze and arrange the kumquat slices on top. Grill for a further 15 minutes until well-browned and cooked through. If they start to brown too quickly, turn down the grill a little.

Remove the skewers and cut each poussin in half along the breastbone. Serve immediately with the salad, crusty bread or new potatoes.

Try this: FOR AN ALTERNATIVE: 248   FOR A VEGETABLE OPTION: 260

Potato–stuffed Roast Poussin

SERVES 4

4 oven-ready poussins
salt and freshly ground
    black pepper
1 lemon, cut into quarters
450 g/1 lb floury potatoes,
    peeled and cut into 4 cm/
    1½ inch pieces

1 tbsp freshly chopped
    thyme or rosemary
3–4 tbsp olive oil
4 garlic cloves, unpeeled
    and lightly smashed
8 slices streaky bacon or
    Parma ham

125 ml/4 fl oz white wine
2 spring onions, trimmed
    and thinly sliced
2 tbsp double cream or
    crème fraîche
lemon wedges, to garnish

Preheat the oven to 220˚C/425˚F/Gas Mark 7. Place a roasting tin in the oven to heat. Rinse the poussin cavities and pat dry with absorbent kitchen paper. Season the cavities with salt and pepper and a squeeze of lemon. Push a lemon quarter into each cavity.

Put the potatoes in a saucepan of lightly salted water and bring to the boil. Reduce the heat to low and simmer until just tender; do not overcook. Drain and cool slightly. Sprinkle the chopped herbs over the potatoes and drizzle with 2–3 tablespoons of the oil.

Spoon half the potatoes into the poussin cavities – not too tightly. Rub each poussin with a little oil and season with pepper. Carefully spoon 1 tablespoon of oil into the hot roasting tin and arrange the poussins with the remaining potatoes around the edge. Sprinkle over the garlic.

Roast the poussins in the preheated oven for 30 minutes, or until the skin is golden and beginning to crisp. Carefully lay the bacon slices over the breast of each poussin and continue to roast for 15–20 minutes until crisp and the poussins are cooked through. Transfer the poussins and potatoes to a serving platter and cover loosely with tinfoil. Skim off the fat from the juices. Place the tin over a medium heat, add the wine and spring onions. Cook briefly, scraping the bits from the bottom of the tin. Whisk in the cream or crème fraîche and bubble for 1 minute, or until thickened. Garnish the poussins with lemon wedges, and serve with the creamy gravy.

Try this: FOR AN ALTERNATIVE: 246 FOR A VEGETABLE OPTION: 256

Vegetables & Vegetarian

Vegetarian Spaghetti Bolognese

SERVES 4

2 tbsp olive oil
1 onion, peeled and
    finely chopped
1 carrot, peeled and
    finely chopped
1 celery stick, trimmed and
    finely chopped

225 g/8 oz Quorn mince
150 ml/5 fl oz red wine
300 ml/½ pint
    vegetable stock
1 tsp mushroom ketchup
4 tbsp tomato purée
350 g/12 oz dried spaghetti

4 tbsp half-fat crème fraîche
salt and freshly ground
    black pepper
1 tbsp freshly
    chopped parsley

Heat the oil in a large saucepan and add the onion, carrot and celery. Cook gently for 10 minutes, adding a little water if necessary, until softened and starting to brown.

Add the Quorn mince and cook a further 2–3 minutes before adding the red wine. Increase the heat and simmer gently until nearly all the wine has evaporated.

Mix together the vegetable stock and mushroom ketchup and add about half to the Quorn mixture along with the tomato purée. Cover and simmer gently for about 45 minutes, adding the remaining stock as necessary.

Meanwhile, bring a large pan of salted water to the boil and add the spaghetti. Cook until al dente or according to the packet instructions. Drain well. Remove the sauce from the heat, add the crème fraîche and season to taste with salt and pepper. Stir in the parsley and serve immediately with the pasta.

Try this: FOR AN ALTERNATIVE: 276   FOR A MEAT OPTION: 172

Spring Vegetable & Herb Risotto

SERVES 2-3

1 litre/1¾ pint
   vegetable stock
125 g/4 oz asparagus
   tips, trimmed
125 g/4 oz baby
   carrots, scrubbed
50 g/2 oz peas, fresh
   or frozen

50 g/2 oz fine French
   beans, trimmed
1 tbsp olive oil
1 onion, peeled and
   finely chopped
1 garlic clove, peeled and
   finely chopped
2 tsp freshly chopped thyme

225 g/8 oz risotto rice
150 ml/¼ pint white wine
1 tbsp each freshly chopped
   basil, chives and parsley
zest of ½ lemon
3 tbsp half-fat crème fraîche
salt and freshly ground
   black pepper

Bring the vegetable stock to the boil in a large saucepan and add the asparagus, baby carrots, peas and beans. Bring the stock back to the boil and remove the vegetables at once using a slotted spoon. Rinse under cold running water. Drain again and reserve. Keep the stock hot.

Heat the oil in a large deep frying pan and add the onion. Cook over a medium heat for 4–5 minutes until starting to brown. Add the garlic and thyme and cook for a further few seconds. Add the rice and stir well for a minute until the rice is hot and coated in oil.

Add the white wine and stir constantly until the wine is almost completely absorbed by the rice. Begin adding the stock a ladleful at a time, stirring well and waiting until the last ladleful has been absorbed before stirring in the next. Add the vegetables after using about half of the stock. Continue until all the stock is used. This will take 20–25 minutes. The rice and vegetables should both be tender.

Remove the pan from the heat. Stir in the herbs, lemon zest and crème fraîche. Season to taste with salt and pepper and serve immediately.

Try this: FOR AN ALTERNATIVE: 282   FOR A MEAT OPTION: 146

Roasted Mixed Vegetables with Garlic & Herb Sauce

SERVES 4

1 large garlic bulb
1 large onion, peeled
    and cut into wedges
4 small carrots, peeled
    and quartered
4 small parsnips, peeled
6 small potatoes, scrubbed

    and halved
1 fennel bulb, sliced thickly
4 sprigs of fresh rosemary
4 sprigs of fresh thyme
2 tbsp olive oil
salt and freshly ground
    black pepper

200 g/7 oz low-fat soft
    cheese with herbs
    and garlic
4 tbsp milk
zest of ½ lemon
sprigs of thyme,
    to garnish

Preheat the oven to 220°C/425°F/Gas Mark 7. Cut the garlic in half horizontally. Put into a large roasting tin with all the vegetables and herbs.

Add the oil, season well with salt and pepper and toss together to coat lightly in the oil.

Cover with tinfoil and roast in the preheated oven for 50 minutes. Remove the tinfoil and cook for a further 30 minutes until all the vegetables are tender and slightly charred.

Remove the tin from the oven and allow to cool.

In a small saucepan, melt the low-fat soft cheese together with the milk and lemon zest.

Remove the garlic from the roasting tin and squeeze the flesh into a bowl. Mash thoroughly then add to the sauce. Heat through gently. Season the vegetables to taste. Pour some sauce into small ramekins and garnish with 4 sprigs of thyme. Serve immediately with the roasted vegetables and the sauce to dip.

Try this: FOR AN ALTERNATIVE: 258   FOR A MEAT OPTION: 144

Vegetable Cassoulet

SERVES 6

125 g/4 oz dried haricot
beans, soaked overnight
2 tbsp olive oil
2 garlic cloves, peeled
and chopped
225 g/8 oz baby onions,
peeled and halved
2 carrots, peeled and diced
2 celery sticks, trimmed and

finely chopped
1 red pepper, deseeded
and chopped
175 g/6 oz mixed
mushrooms, sliced
1 tbsp each freshly chopped
rosemary, thyme
and sage
150 ml/¼ pint red wine

4 tbsp tomato purée
1 tbsp dark soy sauce
salt and freshly ground
black pepper
50 g/2 oz fresh breadcrumbs
1 tbsp freshly
chopped parsley
basil sprigs, to garnish

Preheat the oven to 190˚C/375˚F/Gas Mark 5. Drain the haricot beans and place in
a saucepan with 1.1 litres/2 pints of fresh water. Bring to the boil and boil rapidly for
10 minutes. Reduce the heat and simmer gently for 45 minutes. Drain the beans, reserving
300 ml/½ pint of the liquid.

Heat 1 tablespoon of the oil in a flameproof casserole and add the garlic, onions, carrot,
celery and red pepper. Cook gently for 10–12 minutes until tender and starting to brown.
Add a little water if the vegetables start to stick. Add the mushrooms and cook for a further
5 minutes until softened. Add the herbs and stir briefly.

Stir in the red wine and boil rapidly for about 5 minutes until reduced and syrupy. Stir in the
reserved beans and their liquid, tomato purée and soy sauce. Season to taste with salt and pepper.

Mix together the breadcrumbs and parsley with the remaining 1 tablespoon of oil. Scatter this
mixture evenly over the top of the stew. Cover loosely with foil and transfer to the preheated
oven. Cook for 30 minutes. Carefully remove the foil and cook for a further 15–20 minutes
until the topping is crisp and golden. Serve immediately, garnished with basil sprigs.

Try this: FOR AN ALTERNATIVE: 256   FOR A MEAT OPTION: 154

Ratatouille

SERVES 4

1 red pepper
2 courgettes, trimmed
1 small aubergine, trimmed
1 onion, peeled

2 ripe tomatoes
50 g/2 oz button
   mushrooms, wiped
   and halved or quartered

200 ml/7 fl oz tomato juice
1 tbsp freshly chopped basil
salt and freshly ground
   black pepper

Deseed the peppers, remove the membrane with a small sharp knife and cut into small dice. Thickly slice the courgettes and cut the aubergine into small dice. Slice the onion into rings.

Place the tomatoes in boiling water until their skins begin to peel away. Remove the skins from the tomatoes, cut into quarters and remove the seeds.

Place all the vegetables in a saucepan with the tomato juice and basil. Season to taste with salt and pepper.

Bring to the boil, cover and simmer for 15 minutes or until the vegetables are tender. Remove the vegetables with a slotted spoon and arrange in a serving dish.

Bring the liquid in the pan to the boil and boil for 20 seconds until it is slightly thickened. Season the sauce to taste with salt and pepper.

Pass the sauce through a sieve to remove some of the seeds and pour over the vegetables. Serve the ratatouille hot or cold.

Try this: FOR AN ALTERNATIVE: 262 FOR A MEAT OPTION: 152

Mushroom Stew

SERVES 4

15 g/½ oz dried
  porcini mushrooms
900 g/2 lb assorted fresh
  mushrooms, wiped
2 tbsp good quality
  virgin olive oil
1 onion, peeled and
  finely chopped

2 garlic cloves, peeled and
  finely chopped
1 tbsp fresh thyme leaves
pinch of ground cloves
salt and freshly ground
  black pepper
700 g/1½ lb tomatoes,
  peeled, deseeded

  and chopped
225 g/8 oz instant polenta
600ml/1 pint vegetable stock
3 tbsp freshly chopped
  mixed herbs
sprigs of parsley,
  to garnish

Soak the porcini mushrooms in a small bowl of hot water for 20 minutes. Drain reserving the porcini mushrooms and their soaking liquor. Cut the fresh mushrooms in half and reserve.

In a saucepan, heat the oil and add the onion. Cook gently for 5–7 minutes until softened. Add the garlic, thyme and cloves and continue cooking for 2 minutes.

Add all the mushrooms and cook for 8–10 minutes until the mushrooms have softened, stirring often. Season to taste with salt and pepper and add the tomatoes and the reserved soaking liquid. Simmer, partly-covered, over a low heat for about 20 minutes until thickened. Adjust the seasoning to taste.

Meanwhile, cook the polenta according to the packet instructions using the vegetable stock. Stir in the herbs and divide between four dishes. Ladle the mushrooms over the polenta, garnish with the parsley and serve immediately.

Try this: FOR AN ALTERNATIVE: 260   FOR A MEAT OPTION: 182

Stuffed Tomatoes with Grilled Polenta

SERVES 4

For the polenta:
300 ml/½ pint vegetable
    stock
salt and freshly ground
    black pepper
50 g/2 oz quick-cook polenta
15 g/½ oz butter

For the stuffed tomatoes:
4 large tomatoes
1 tbsp olive oil
1 garlic clove, peeled
    and crushed
1 bunch spring onions,
    trimmed and
    finely chopped

2 tbsp freshly chopped
    parsley
2 tbsp freshly chopped basil
2 slices Parma ham, cut into
    thin slivers
50 g/2 oz fresh white
    breadcrumbs
snipped chives, to garnish

Preheat grill just before cooking. To make the polenta, pour the stock into a saucepan. Add a pinch of salt and bring to the boil. Pour in the polenta in a fine stream, stirring all the time. Simmer for about 15 minutes, or until very thick. Stir in the butter and add a little pepper. Turn the polenta out on to a chopping board and spread to a thickness of just over 1 cm/½ inch. Cool, cover with clingfilm and chill in the refrigerator for 30 minutes.

To make the stuffed tomatoes, cut the tomatoes in half then scoop out the seeds and press through a fine sieve to extract the juices. Season the insides of the tomatoes with salt and pepper and reserve. Heat the olive oil in a saucepan and gently fry the garlic and spring onions for 3 minutes. Add the tomatoes' juices, bubble for 3–4 minutes, until most of the liquid has evaporated. Stir in the herbs, Parma ham and a little black pepper with half the breadcrumbs. Spoon into the hollowed out tomatoes and reserve.

Cut the polenta into 5 cm/2 inch squares, then cut again to make triangles. Put the triangles on a piece of tinfoil on the grill rack and grill for 4–5 minutes on each side, until golden. Cover and keep warm. Grill the tomatoes under a medium-hot grill for about 4 minutes – any exposed Parma ham will become crisp. Sprinkle with the remaining breadcrumbs and grill for 1–2 minutes, or until the breadcrumbs are golden brown. Garnish with snipped chives and serve immediately with the grilled polenta.

Try this: FOR AN ALTERNATIVE: 266   FOR A MEAT OPTION: 178

Rice–filled Peppers

SERVES 4

8 ripe tomatoes
2 tbsp olive oil
1 onion, peeled and
    chopped
1 garlic clove, peeled
    and crushed

½ tsp dark muscovado sugar
125 g/4 oz cooked
    long-grain rice
50 g/2 oz pine nuts, toasted
1 tbsp freshly chopped
    oregano

salt and freshly ground
    black pepper
2 large red peppers
2 large yellow peppers
mixed salad, to serve
crusty bread, to serve

Preheat oven to 200°C/400°F/Gas Mark 6. Put the tomatoes in a small bowl and pour over boiling water to cover. Leave for 1 minute, then drain. Plunge the tomatoes into cold water to cool, then peel off the skins. Quarter, remove the seeds and chop.

Heat the olive oil in a frying pan, and cook the onion gently for 10 minutes, until softened. Add the garlic, chopped tomatoes and sugar.

Gently cook the tomato mixture for 10 minutes until thickened. Remove from the heat and stir the rice, pine nuts and oregano into the sauce. Season to taste with salt and pepper.

Halve the peppers lengthways, cutting through and leaving the stem on. Remove the seeds and cores, then put the peppers in a lightly oiled roasting tin, cut-side down and cook in the preheated oven for about 10 minutes.

Turn the peppers so they are cut side up. Spoon in the filling, then cover with tinfoil. Return to the oven for 15 minutes, or until the peppers are very tender, removing the tinfoil for the last 5 minutes to allow the tops to brown a little.

Serve 1 red pepper half and 1 yellow pepper half per person with a mixed salad and plenty of warmed, crusty bread.

Try this: FOR AN ALTERNATIVE: 264   FOR A MEAT OPTION: 156

Baby Roast Potato Salad

SERVES 4

350 g/12 oz small shallots
sea salt and freshly ground
  black pepper
900 g/2 lb small even-sized
  new potatoes

2 tbsp olive oil
2 medium courgettes
2 sprigs of fresh rosemary
175 g/6 oz cherry tomatoes
150 ml/¼ pint soured cream

2 tbsp freshly
  snipped chives
¼ tsp paprika

Preheat the oven to 200°C/400°F/Gas Mark 6. Trim the shallots, but leave the skins on. Put in a saucepan of lightly salted boiling water with the potatoes and cook for 5 minutes; drain. Separate the shallots and plunge them into cold water for 1 minute.

Put the oil in a baking sheet lined with tinfoil or roasting tin and heat for a few minutes. Peel the skins off the shallots – they should now come away easily. Add to the baking sheet or roasting tin with the potatoes and toss in the oil to coat. Sprinkle with a little sea salt. Roast the potatoes and shallots in the preheated oven for 10 minutes.

Meanwhile, trim the courgettes, halve lengthways and cut into 5 cm/2 inch chunks. Add to the baking sheet or roasting tin, toss to mix and cook for 5 minutes.

Pierce the tomato skins with a sharp knife. Add to the sheet or tin with the rosemary and cook for a further 5 minutes, or until all the vegetables are tender. Remove the rosemary and discard. Grind a little black pepper over the vegetables.

Spoon into a wide serving bowl. Mix together the soured cream and chives and drizzle over the vegetables just before serving.

Try this: FOR AN ALTERNATIVE: 270 FOR A MEAT OPTION: 124

Warm Potato, Pear &
Pecan Salad

SERVES 4

900 g/2 lb new potatoes,
 preferably red-skinned,
 unpeeled
salt and freshly ground
 black pepper

1 tsp Dijon mustard
2 tsp white wine vinegar
3 tbsp groundnut oil
1 tbsp hazelnut or walnut oil
2 tsp poppy seeds

2 firm ripe dessert pears
2 tsp lemon juice
175 g/6 oz baby
 spinach leaves
75 g/3 oz toasted pecan nuts

Scrub the potatoes, then cook in a saucepan of lightly salted boiling water for 15 minutes, or until tender. Drain, cut into halves, or quarters if large, and place in a serving bowl.

In a small bowl or jug, whisk together the mustard and vinegar. Gradually add the oils until the mixture begins to thicken. Stir in the poppy seeds and season to taste with salt and pepper.

Pour about two-thirds of the dressing over the hot potatoes and toss gently to coat. Leave until the potatoes have soaked up the dressing and are just warm.

Meanwhile, quarter and core the pears. Cut into thin slices, then sprinkle with the lemon juice to prevent them from going brown. Add to the potatoes with the spinach leaves and toasted pecan nuts. Gently mix together.

Drizzle the remaining dressing over the salad. Serve immediately before the spinach starts to wilt.

Try this: FOR AN ALTERNATIVE: 268 FOR A MEAT OPTION: 224

Vegetable Frittata

SERVES 2

6 medium eggs
2 tbsp freshly chopped
    parsley
1 tbsp freshly chopped
    tarragon
25 g/1 oz pecorino or
    Parmesan cheese,

finely grated
freshly ground black pepper
175 g/6 oz tiny new potatoes
2 small carrots, peeled
    and sliced
125 g/4 oz broccoli, cut into
    small florets

1 courgette, about
    125 g/4 oz, sliced
2 tbsp olive oil
4 spring onions, trimmed
    and thinly sliced
mixed green salad, to serve
crusty Italian bread, to serve

Preheat grill just before cooking. Lightly beat the eggs with the parsley, tarragon and half the cheese. Season to taste with black pepper and reserve. (Salt is not needed as the pecorino is very salty.)

Bring a large saucepan of lightly salted water to the boil. Add the new potatoes and cook for 8 minutes. Add the carrots and cook for 4 minutes, then add the broccoli florets and the courgettes and cook for a further 3–4 minutes, or until all the vegetables are barely tender. Drain well.

Heat the oil in a 20.5 cm/8 inch heavy-based frying pan. Add the spring onions and cook for 3–4 minutes, or until softened. Add all the vegetables and cook for a few seconds, then pour in the beaten egg mixture. Stir gently for about a minute, then cook for a further 1–2 minutes, or until the bottom of the frittata is set and golden brown.

Place the pan under a hot grill for 1 minute, or until almost set and just beginning to brown. Sprinkle with the remaining cheese and grill for a further 1 minute, or until it is lightly browned.

Loosen the edges and slide out of the pan. Cut into wedges and serve hot or warm with a mixed green salad and crusty Italian bread.

Try this: FOR AN ALTERNATIVE: 290 FOR A MEAT OPTION: 158

Cheesy Pasta with Tomatoes & Cream

SERVES 4

225 g/8 oz fresh ricotta cheese
225 g/8 oz smoked
mozzarella, grated, (use
normal if smoked is
unavailable)
5 g/4 oz freshly
grated pecorino or
Parmesan cheese
2 medium eggs, lightly beaten

2–3 tbsp finely chopped
mint, basil or parsley
salt and freshly ground
black pepper

For the sauce:
2 tbsp olive oil
1 small onion, peeled and
finely chopped

2 garlic cloves, peeled and
finely chopped
450g/1 lb ripe plum
tomatoes, peeled,
deseeded and finely
chopped
50 ml/2 fl oz white vermouth
225 ml/8 fl oz double cream
fresh basil leaves, to garnish

Place the ricotta cheese in a bowl and beat until smooth, then add the remaining cheeses with the eggs, herbs and seasoning to taste. Beat well until creamy and smooth.

Cut the prepared pasta dough into quarters. Working with one-quarter at a time, and covering the remaining quarters with a clean, damp tea towel, roll out the pasta very thinly. Using a 10 cm/4 inch pastry cutter or small saucer, cut out as many rounds as possible.

Place a small tablespoonful of the filling mixture slightly below the centre of each round. Lightly moisten the edge of the round with water and fold in half to form a filled half-moon shape. Using a dinner fork, press the edges together firmly. Transfer to a lightly floured baking sheet and continue filling the remaining pasta. Leave to dry for 15 minutes.

Heat the oil in a large saucepan, add the onions and cook for 3–4 minutes, or until beginning to soften. Add the garlic and cook for 1–2 minutes, then add the tomatoes, vermouth and cream and bring to the boil. Simmer for 10–15 minutes, or until thickened and reduced. Bring a large saucepan of salted water to the boil. Add the filled pasta and return to the boil. Cook, stirring frequently to prevent sticking, for 5 minutes, or until 'al dente'. Drain and return to the pan. Pour over the tomato and cream sauce, garnish with basil leaves and serve immediately

Try this: FOR AN ALTERNATIVE: 280   FOR A MEAT OPTION: 160

Four–cheese Tagliatelle

SERVES 4

300 ml/½ pint
  whipping cream
4 garlic cloves, peeled
  and lightly bruised
75 g/3 oz fontina
  cheese, diced
75 g/3 oz Gruyère

cheese, grated
75 g/3 oz mozzarella cheese,
  preferably, diced
50 g/2 oz Parmesan cheese,
  grated, plus extra
  to serve
salt and freshly ground

black pepper
275 g/10 oz fresh
  green tagliatelle
1–2 tbsp freshly
  snipped chives
fresh basil leaves,
  to garnish

Place the whipping cream with the garlic cloves in a medium pan and heat gently until small bubbles begin to form around the edge of the pan. Using a slotted spoon, remove and discard the garlic cloves.

Add all the cheeses to the pan and stir until melted. Season with a little salt and a lot of black pepper. Keep the sauce warm over a low heat, but do not allow to boil.

Meanwhile, bring a large pan of lightly salted water to the boil. Add the taglietelle, return to the boil and cook for 2–3 minutes, or until 'al dente'.

Drain the pasta thoroughly and return to the pan. Pour the sauce over the pasta, add the chives then toss lightly until well coated. Tip into a warmed serving dish or spoon on to individual plates. Garnish with a few basil leaves and serve immediately with extra Parmesan cheese.

Try this: FOR AN ALTERNATIVE: 274   FOR A MEAT OPTION: 174

Courgette Lasagne

SERVES 8

2 tbsp olive oil
1 medium onion, peeled
  and finely chopped
225 g/8 oz mushrooms,
  wiped and thinly sliced
3–4 courgettes, trimmed
  and thinly sliced
2 garlic cloves, peeled

and finely chopped
½ tsp dried thyme
1–2 tbsp freshly chopped
  basil or flat-leaf parsley
salt and freshly ground
  black pepper
1 quantity prepared white
  sauce (see page 170)

350 g/12 oz lasagne
  sheets, cooked
225 g/8 oz mozzarella
  cheese, grated
50 g/2 oz Parmesan
  cheese, grated
400 g can chopped
  tomatoes, drained

Preheat the oven to 200°C/400°F/Gas Mark 6, 15 minutes before cooking. Heat the oil in a large frying pan, add the onion and cook for 3–5 minutes. Add the mushrooms, cook for 2 minutes then add the courgettes and cook for a further 3–4 minutes, or until tender. Stir in the garlic, thyme and basil or parsley and season to taste with salt and pepper. Remove from the heat and reserve.

Spoon one-third of the white sauce on to the base of a lightly oiled large baking dish. Arrange a layer of lasagne over the sauce. Spread half the courgette mixture over the pasta, then sprinkle with some of the mozzarella and some of the Parmesan cheese. Repeat with more white sauce and another layer of lasagne, then cover with half the drained tomatoes.

Cover the tomatoes with lasagne, the remaining courgette mixture, and some mozzarella and Parmesan cheese. Repeat the layers ending with a layer of lasagne sheets, white sauce and the remaining Parmesan cheese. Bake in the preheated oven for 35 minutes, or until golden. Serve immediately.

Try this: FOR AN ALTERNATIVE: 294   FOR A MEAT OPTION: 170

Baked Macaroni Cheese

SERVES 8

450 g/1 lb macaroni
75 g/3 oz butter
1 onion, peeled and
    finely chopped
40 g/1½ oz plain flour
1 litre/1¾ pints milk
1–2 dried bay leaves
½ tsp dried thyme

salt and freshly ground
    black pepper
cayenne pepper
freshly grated nutmeg
2 small leeks, trimmed,
    finely chopped, cooked
    and drained
1 tbsp Dijon mustard

400 g/14 oz mature
    Cheddar cheese, grated
2 tbsp dried breadcrumbs
2 tbsp freshly grated
    Parmesan cheese
basil sprig, to garnish

Preheat the oven to 190°C/375°F/Gas Mark 5, 10 minutes before cooking. Bring a large pan of lightly salted water to a rolling boil. Add the macaroni and cook according to the packet instructions, or until 'al dente'. Drain thoroughly and reserve.

Meanwhile, melt 50 g/2 oz of the butter in a large, heavy-based saucepan, add the onion and cook, stirring frequently, for 5–7 minutes, or until softened. Sprinkle in the flour and cook, stirring constantly, for 2 minutes. Remove the pan from the heat, stir in the milk, return to the heat and cook, stirring, until a smooth sauce has formed.

Add the bay leaf and thyme to the sauce and season to taste with salt, pepper, cayenne pepper and freshly grated nutmeg. Simmer for about 15 minutes, stirring frequently, until thickened and smooth.

Remove the sauce from the heat. Add the cooked leeks, mustard and Cheddar cheese and stir until the cheese has melted. Stir in the macaroni then tip into a lightly oiled baking dish.

Sprinkle the breadcrumbs and Parmesan cheese over the macaroni. Dot with the remaining butter, then bake in the preheated oven for 1 hour, or until golden. Garnish with a basil sprig and serve immediately.

Try this: FOR AN ALTERNATIVE: 276   FOR A MEAT OPTION: 172

Chinese Egg Fried Rice

SERVES 4

250 g/9 oz long-grain rice
1 tbsp dark sesame oil
2 large eggs
1 tbsp sunflower oil
2 garlic cloves,
    peeled and crushed
2.5 cm/1 inch piece
    fresh root ginger,

peeled and grated
1 carrot, peeled and
    cut into matchsticks
125 g/4 oz mangetout,
    halved
220 g can water chestnuts,
    drained and halved
1 yellow pepper,

deseeded and diced
4 spring onions, trimmed
    and finely shredded
2 tbsp light soy sauce
½ tsp paprika
salt and freshly ground
    black pepper

Bring a saucepan of lightly salted water to the boil, add the rice and cook for 15 minutes or according to the packet instructions. Drain and leave to cool.

Heat a wok or large frying pan and add the sesame oil. Beat the eggs in a small bowl and pour into the hot wok. Using a fork, draw the egg in from the sides of the pan to the centre until it sets, then turn over and cook the other side. When set and golden turn out on to a board. Leave to cool, then cut into very thin strips.

Wipe the wok clean with absorbent kitchen paper, return to the heat and add the sunflower oil. When hot add the garlic and ginger and stir-fry for 30 seconds. Add the remaining vegetables and continue to stir-fry for 3–4 minutes, or until tender but still crisp.

Stir the reserved cooked rice into the wok with the soy sauce and paprika and season to taste with salt and pepper. Fold in the cooked egg strips and heat through. Tip into a warmed serving dish and serve immediately.

Try this: FOR AN ALTERNATIVE: 254   FOR A MEAT OPTION: 146

Mixed Vegetables Stir Fry

SERVES 4

2 tbsp groundnut oil
4 garlic cloves, peeled
   and finely sliced
2.5 cm/1 inch piece fresh
   root ginger, peeled and
   finely sliced
75 g/3 oz broccoli florets
50 g/2 oz mangetout,

trimmed
75 g/3 oz carrots, peeled and
   cut into matchsticks
1 green pepper, deseeded
   and cut into strips
1 red pepper, deseeded and
   cut into strips
1 tbsp soy sauce

1 tbsp hoisin sauce
1 tsp sugar
salt and freshly ground
   black pepper
4 spring onions, trimmed
   and shredded,
   to garnish

Heat a wok, add the oil and when hot, add the garlic and ginger slices and stir-fry for 1 minute.

Add the broccoli florets to the wok, stir-fry for 1 minute, then add the mangetout, carrots and the green and red peppers and stir-fry for a further 3–4 minutes, or until tender but still crisp.

Blend the soy sauce, hoisin sauce and sugar in a small bowl. Stir well, season to taste with salt and pepper and pour into the wok. Transfer the vegetables to a warmed serving dish. Garnish with shredded spring onions and serve immediately.

Try this: FOR AN ALTERNATIVE: 258   FOR A MEAT OPTION: 156

Creamy Vegetable Korma

SERVES 4–6

2 tbsp ghee or vegetable oil
1 large onion, peeled
   and chopped
2 garlic cloves, peeled
   and crushed
2.5 cm/1 inch piece of root
   ginger, peeled and grated
4 cardamom pods
2 tsp ground coriander
1 tsp ground cumin

1 tsp ground turmeric
finely grated rind and juice
   of ½ lemon
50 g/2 oz ground almonds
400 ml/14 fl oz vegetable
   stock
450 g/1 lb potatoes, peeled
   and diced
450 g/1 lb mixed vegetables,
   such as cauliflower,

   carrots and turnip,
   cut into chunks
150 ml/¼ pint double cream
3 tbsp freshly
   chopped coriander
salt and freshly ground
   black pepper
naan bread, to serve

Heat the ghee or oil in a large saucepan. Add the onion and cook for 5 minutes. Stir in the garlic and ginger and cook for a further 5 minutes, or until soft and just beginning to colour.

Stir in the cardamom, ground coriander, cumin and turmeric. Continue cooking over a low heat for 1 minute, stirring.

Stir in the lemon rind and juice and almonds. Blend in the vegetable stock. Slowly bring to the boil, stirring occasionally.

Add the potatoes and vegetables. Bring back to the boil, then reduce the heat, cover and simmer for 35–40 minutes, or until the vegetables are just tender. Check after 25 minutes and add a little more stock if needed.

Slowly stir in the cream and chopped coriander. Season to taste with salt and pepper. Cook very gently until heated through, but do not boil. Serve immediately with naan bread.

Try this: FOR AN ALTERNATIVE: 262   FOR A MEAT OPTION: 182

Red Pepper & Basil Tart

SERVES 4-6

For the olive pastry:
225 g/8 oz plain flour
pinch of salt
50 g/2 oz pitted black olives,
   finely chopped
1 medium egg, lightly
   beaten, plus 1 egg yolk
3 tbsp olive oil

For the filling:
2 large red peppers,
   quartered and deseeded
175 g/6 oz mascarpone
   cheese
4 tbsp milk
2 medium eggs
3 tbsp freshly chopped basil

salt and freshly ground
   black pepper
sprig of fresh basil,
to garnish
mixed salad, to serve

Preheat the oven to 200°C/400°F/Gas Mark 6, 15 minutes before cooking. Sift the flour and salt into a bowl. Make a well in the centre. Stir together the egg, oil and 1 tablespoon of tepid water. Add to the dry ingredients, drop in the olives and mix to a dough. Knead on a lightly floured surface for a few seconds until smooth, then wrap in clingfilm and chill in the refrigerator for 30 minutes.

Roll out the pastry and use to line a 23 cm/9 inch loose-bottomed fluted flan tin. Lightly prick the base with a fork. Cover and chill in the refrigerator for 20 minutes. Cook the peppers under a hot grill for 10 minutes, or until the skins are blackened and blistered. Put the peppers in a plastic bag, cool for 10 minutes, then remove the skin and slice.

Line the pastry case with tinfoil or greaseproof paper weighed down with baking beans and bake in the preheated oven for 10 minutes. Remove the tinfoil and beans and bake for a further 5 minutes. Reduce the oven temperature to 180°C/350°F/Gas Mark 4. Beat the mascarpone cheese until smooth. Gradually add the milk and eggs. Stir in the peppers, basil and season to taste with salt and pepper. Spoon into the flan case and bake for 25–30 minutes, or until lightly set. Garnish with a sprig of fresh basil and serve immediately with a mixed salad.

Try this: FOR AN ALTERNATIVE: 290   FOR A MEAT OPTION: 156

Stilton, Tomato & Courgette Quiche

SERVES 4

1 quantity shortcrust pastry
(see page 90)
2 large eggs, beaten
25 g/1 oz butter
1 onion, peeled and

finely chopped
1 courgette, trimmed and
sliced
125 g/4 oz Stilton
cheese, crumbled

6 cherry tomatoes, halved
200 ml tub crème fraîche
salt and freshly ground
black pepper

Preheat the oven to 190°C/375°F/Gas Mark 5. On a lightly floured surface, roll out the pastry and use to line an 18 cm/7 inch lightly oiled quiche or flan tin, trimming any excess pastry with a knife.

Prick the base all over with a fork and bake blind in the preheated oven for 15 minutes. Remove the pastry from the oven and brush with a little of the beaten egg. Return to the oven for a further 5 minutes.

Heat the butter in a frying pan and gently fry the onion and courgette for about 4 minutes until soft and starting to brown. Transfer into the pastry case.

Sprinkle the Stilton over evenly and top with the halved cherry tomatoes. Beat together the eggs and crème fraîche and season to taste with salt and pepper.

Pour the filling into the pastry case and bake in the oven for 35–40 minutes, or until the filling is golden brown and set in the centre. Serve the quiche hot or cold.

Try this: FOR AN ALTERNATIVE: 294   FOR A MEAT OPTION: 168

Roasted Vegetable Pie

SERVES 4

225 g/8 oz plain flour
pinch of salt
50 g/2 oz white vegetable fat
 or lard, cut into squares
50 g/2 oz butter, cut into
 squares
2 tsp herbes de Provence
1 red pepper, deseeded and
 halved

1 green pepper, deseeded
 and halved
1 yellow pepper, deseeded
 and halved
3 tbsp extra-virgin olive oil
1 aubergine, trimmed,
 and sliced
1 courgette, trimmed and
 cut into chunks

1 leek, trimmed and
 cut into chunks
1 medium egg, beaten
125 g/4 oz fresh mozzarella
 cheese, sliced
salt and freshly ground
 black pepper
sprigs of mixed herbs,
 to garnish

Preheat the oven to 220˚C/425˚F/Gas Mark 7. Sift the flour and salt into a large bowl, add the fats and mix lightly. Using the fingertips rub into the flour until it resembles breadcrumbs. Stir in the herbes de Provence. Sprinkle over a tablespoon of cold water and with a knife start bringing the dough together. (Perhaps using the hands for the final stage.) If the dough does not form a ball instantly, add a little more water. Place in a polythene bag and chill for 30 minutes.

Place the peppers on a baking tray and sprinkle with 1 tablespoon of oil. Roast in the preheated oven for 20 minutes or until the skins start to blacken. Brush the aubergines, courgettes and leeks with oil and place on another baking tray. Roast in the oven with the peppers for 20 minutes. Place the blackened peppers in a polythene bag and leave the skin to loosen for 5 minutes. When cool enough to handle, peel the skins off the peppers.

Roll out half the pastry on a lightly floured surface and use to line a 20.5 cm/8 inch round pie dish. Line the pastry with greaseproof paper and fill with baking beans or rice and bake blind for about 10 minutes. Remove the beans and the paper, then brush the base with a little of the beaten egg. Return to the oven for 5 minutes. Layer the cooked vegetables and the cheese in the pastry case, seasoning each layer. Roll out the remaining pastry, and cut out the lid 5 mm/¼ inch wider than the dish. Brush the rim with the beaten egg and lay the pastry on top, press to seal. Knock the edges with the back of a knife. Cut a slit in the lid and brush with the beaten egg. Bake for 30 minutes. Transfer to a large serving dish, garnish and serve immediately.

Try this: FOR AN ALTERNATIVE: 256   FOR A MEAT OPTION: 184

Tomato & Courgette Herb Tart

SERVES 4

4 tbsp olive oil
1 onion, peeled and
    finely chopped
3 garlic cloves, peeled
and crushed
400 g/14 oz prepared puff

pastry, thawed if frozen
1 small egg, beaten
2 tbsp freshly
    chopped rosemary
2 tbsp freshly
    chopped parsley

175 g/6 oz rindless fresh
    soft goats' cheese
4 ripe plum tomatoes, sliced
1 medium courgette,
    trimmed and sliced
thyme sprigs, to garnish

Preheat the oven to 230°C/450°F/Gas Mark 8. Heat 2 tablespoons of the oil in a large frying pan.
Fry the onion and garlic for about 4 minutes until softened and reserve.

Roll out the pastry on a lightly floured surface, and cut out a 30.5 cm/12 inch circle. Brush
the pastry with a little beaten egg, then prick all over with a fork. Transfer on to a dampened
baking sheet and bake in the preheated oven for 10 minutes.

Turn the pastry over and brush with a little more egg. Bake for 5 more minutes,
then remove from the oven.

Mix together the onion, garlic and herbs with the goats' cheese and spread over the pastry.
Arrange the tomatoes and courgettes over the goats' cheese and drizzle with the remaining oil.

Bake for 20–25 minutes, or until the pastry is golden brown and the topping bubbling. Garnish
with the thyme sprigs and serve immediately.

Try this: FOR AN ALTERNATIVE: 290   FOR A MEAT OPTION: 180

Leek & Potato Tart

SERVES 6

225 g/8 oz plain flour
pinch of salt
150 g/5 oz butter, cubed
50 g/2 oz walnuts, very finely
    chopped
1 large egg yolk

For the filling:
450 g/1 lb leeks, trimmed
    and thinly sliced
40 g/1½ oz butter
450 g/1 lb large new
    potatoes, scrubbed
300 ml/½ pint soured cream

3 medium eggs, lightly
    beaten
175 g/6 oz Gruyère cheese,
    grated
freshly grated nutmeg
salt and freshly ground
    black pepper
fresh chives, to garnish

Preheat the oven to 200°C/400°F/Gas Mark 6, about 15 minutes before baking. Sift the flour and salt into a bowl. Rub in the butter until the mixture resembles breadcrumbs. Stir in the nuts. Mix together the egg yolk and 3 tablespoons of cold water. Sprinkle over the dry ingredients. Mix to form a dough. Knead on a lightly floured surface for a few seconds, then wrap in clingfilm and chill in the refrigerator for 20 minutes. Roll out and use to line a 20.5 cm/8 inch spring-form tin or very deep flan tin. Chill for a further 30 minutes.

Cook the leeks in the butter over a high heat for 2–3 minutes, stirring constantly. Lower the heat, cover and cook for 25 minutes until soft, stirring occasionally. Remove the leeks from the heat.

Cook the potatoes in boiling salted water for 15 minutes, or until almost tender. Drain and thickly slice. Add to the leeks. Stir the soured cream into the leeks and potatoes, followed by the eggs, cheese, nutmeg and salt and pepper. Pour into the pastry case and bake on the middle shelf in the preheated oven for 20 minutes.

Reduce the oven temperature to 190°C/375°F/Gas Mark 5 and cook for a further 30–35 minutes, or until the filling is set. Garnish with chives and serve immediately.

Try this: FOR AN ALTERNATIVE: 270   FOR A MEAT OPTION: 120

Puddings & Desserts

Rice Pudding

SERVES 4

60 g/2½ oz pudding rice
50 g/2 oz granulated sugar
410 g can light
   evaporated milk

300 ml/½ pint semi-
   skimmed milk
pinch of freshly
   grated nutmeg

25 g/1 oz half-fat butter
reduced sugar jam,
   to decorate

Preheat the oven to 150°C/300°F/Gas Mark 2. Lightly oil a large ovenproof dish.

Sprinkle the rice and the sugar into the dish and mix.

Bring the evaporated milk and milk to the boil in a small pan, stirring occasionally. Stir the milks into the rice and mix well until the rice is coated thoroughly. Sprinkle over the nutmeg, cover with tinfoil and bake in the preheated oven for 30 minutes.

Remove the pudding from the oven and stir well, breaking up any lumps. Cover with the same tinfoil. Bake in the preheated oven for a further 30 minutes. Remove from the oven and stir well again. Dot the pudding with butter and bake for a further 45–60 minutes, until the rice is tender and the skin is browned.

Divide the pudding into 4 individual serving bowls. Top with a large spoonful of the jam and serve immediately.

Try this: FOR AN ALTERNATIVE: 330   FOR A MAIN COURSE: 108

Golden Castle Pudding

SERVES 4–6

125 g/4 oz butter
125 g/4 oz caster sugar
a few drops of

vanilla essence
2 medium eggs, beaten
125 g/4 oz self-raising flour

4 tbsp golden syrup
crème fraîche or ready-made
custard, to serve

Preheat the oven to 180°C/350°F/Gas Mark 4. Lightly oil 4–6 individual pudding bowls and place a small circle of lightly oiled non-stick baking or greaseproof paper in the base of each one.

Place the butter and caster sugar in a large bowl, then beat together until the mixture is pale and creamy. Stir in the vanilla essence and gradually add the beaten eggs, a little at a time. Add a tablespoon of flour after each addition of egg and beat well.

When the mixture is smooth, add the remaining flour and fold in gently. Add a tablespoon of water and mix to form a soft mixture that will drop easily off a spoon.

Spoon enough mixture into each basin to come halfway up the tin, allowing enough space for the puddings to rise. Place on a baking sheet and bake in the preheated oven for about 25 minutes until firm and golden brown.

Allow the puddings to stand for 5 minutes. Discard the paper circle and turn out on to individual serving plates.

Warm the golden syrup in a small saucepan and pour a little over each pudding. Serve hot with the crème fraîche or custard.

Try this: FOR AN ALTERNATIVE: 334   FOR A MAIN COURSE: 208

College Pudding

SERVES 4

125 g/4 oz shredded suet
125 g/4 oz fresh
　white breadcrumbs
50 g/2 oz sultanas
50 g/2 oz seedless raisins

½ tsp ground cinnamon
¼ tsp freshly grated nutmeg
¼ tsp mixed spice
50 g/2 oz caster sugar
½ tsp baking powder

2 medium eggs, beaten
orange zest, to garnish

Preheat the oven to 180°C/350°F/Gas Mark 4. Lightly oil an ovenproof 900 ml/1½ pint ovenproof pudding basin and place a small circle of greaseproof paper in the base.

Mix the shredded suet and breadcrumbs together and rub lightly together with the fingertips to remove any lumps.

Stir in the dried fruit, spices, sugar and baking powder. Add the eggs and beat lightly together until the mixture is well blended and the fruit is evenly distributed.

Spoon the mixture into the prepared pudding basin and level the surface. Place on a baking tray and cover lightly with some greaseproof paper.

Bake in the preheated oven for 20 minutes, then remove the paper and continue to bake for a further 10–15 minutes, or until the top is firm.

When the pudding is cooked, remove from the oven and carefully turn out on to a warmed serving dish. Decorate with the orange zest and serve immediately.

Try this: FOR AN ALTERNATIVE: 306　FOR A MAIN COURSE: 166

Eve's Pudding

SERVES 6

450 g/1 lb cooking apples
175 g/6 oz blackberries
75 g/3 oz demerara sugar
grated rind of 1 lemon

125 g/4 oz caster sugar
125 g/4 oz butter
few drops of vanilla essence
2 medium eggs, beaten

125 g/4 oz self-raising flour
1 tbsp icing sugar
ready-made custard,
 to serve

Preheat the oven to 180°C/350°F/Gas Mark 4. Oil a 1.1 litre/2 pint baking dish.

Peel, core and slice the apples and place a layer in the base of the prepared dish. Sprinkle over some of the blackberries, a little demerara sugar and lemon zest. Continue to layer the apple and blackberries in this way until all the ingredients have been used.

Cream the sugar and butter together until light and fluffy. Beat in the vanilla essence and then the eggs a little at a time, adding a spoonful of flour after each addition. Fold in the extra flour with a metal spoon or rubber spatula and mix well.

Spread the sponge mixture over the top of the fruit and level with the back of a spoon.

Place the dish on a baking sheet and bake in the preheated oven for 35–40 minutes, or until well risen and golden brown. (To test if the pudding is cooked, press the cooked sponge lightly with a clean finger – if it springs back the sponge is cooked.)

Dust the pudding with a little icing sugar and serve immediately with the custard.

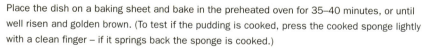

Try this: FOR AN ALTERNATIVE: 316   FOR A MAIN COURSE: 150

Osborne Pudding

SERVES 4

8 slices of white bread
50 g/2 oz butter
2 tbsp marmalade
50 g/2 oz luxury mixed
    dried fruit
2 tbsp fresh orange juice

40 g/1½ oz caster sugar
2 large eggs
450 ml/¾ pint milk
150 ml/¼ pint
    whipping cream

For the marmalade sauce:
zest and juice of 1 orange
2 tbsp thick-cut
    orange marmalade
1 tbsp brandy (optional)
2 tsp cornflour

Preheat the oven to 170°C/325°F/Gas Mark 3. Lightly oil a 1.1 litre/2 pint baking dish.

Remove the crusts from the bread and spread thickly with butter and marmalade. Cut the bread into small triangles. Place half the bread in the base of the dish and sprinkle over the dried mixed fruit, 1 tablespoon of the orange juice and half the caster sugar.

Top with the remaining bread and marmalade, buttered side up and pour over the remaining orange juice. Sprinkle over the remaining caster sugar. Whisk the eggs with the milk and cream and pour over the pudding. Reserve for about 30 minutes to allow the bread to absorb the liquid.

Place in a roasting tin and pour in enough boiling water to come halfway up the sides of the dish. Bake in the preheated oven for 50–60 minutes, or until the pudding is set and the top is crisp and golden.

Meanwhile, make the marmalade sauce. Heat the orange zest and juice with the marmalade and brandy if using. Mix 1 tablespoon of water with the cornflour and mix together well. Add to the saucepan and cook on a low heat, stirring until warmed through and thickened. Serve the pudding hot with the marmalade sauce.

Fruit Salad

SERVES 4

125 g/4 oz caster sugar
3 oranges
700 g/1½ lb lychees,
    peeled and stoned
1 small mango
1 small pineapple
1 papaya

4 pieces stem ginger
    in syrup
4 tbsp stem ginger syrup
125 g/4 oz Cape
    gooseberries
125 g/4 oz strawberries,
    hulled

½ tsp almond essence

To decorate:
lime zest
mint leaves

Place the sugar and 300 ml/½ pint of water in a small pan and heat, gently stirring until the sugar has dissolved. Bring to the boil and simmer for 2 minutes. Once a syrup has formed, remove from the heat and allow to cool.

Using a sharp knife, cut away the skin from the oranges, then slice thickly. Cut each slice in half and place in a serving dish with the syrup and lychees.

Peel the mango, then cut into thick slices around each side of the stone. Discard the stone and cut the slices into bite-sized pieces and add to the syrup.

Using a sharp knife again, carefully cut away the skin from the pineapple. Remove the central core using the knife or an apple corer, then cut the pineapple into segments and add to the syrup.

Peel the papaya, then cut in half and remove the seeds. Cut the flesh into chunks, slice the ginger into matchsticks and add with the ginger syrup to the fruit in the syrup.

Prepare the Cape gooseberries, by removing the thin, papery skins and rinsing lightly. Halve the strawberries, add to the fruit with the almond essence and chill for 30 minutes. Scatter with mint leaves and lime zest to decorate and serve.

Try this: FOR AN ALTERNATIVE: 318   FOR A MAIN COURSE: 230

Lemon & Apricot Pudding

SERVES 4

125 g/4 oz ready-to-eat
dried apricots
3 tbsp orange juice, warmed
50 g/2 oz butter

125 g/4 oz caster sugar
juice and grated rind of
2 lemons
2 medium eggs

50 g/2 oz self-raising flour
300 ml/½ pint milk
custard or fresh cream,
to serve

Preheat the oven to 180°C/350°F/Gas Mark 4. Oil a 1.1 litre/2 pint pie dish.

Soak the apricots in the orange juice for 10–15 minutes or until most of the juice has been absorbed, then place in the base of the pie dish.

Cream the butter and sugar together with the lemon rind until light and fluffy.

Separate the eggs. Beat the egg yolks into the creamed mixture with a spoonful of flour after each addition. Add the remaining flour and beat well until smooth.

Stir the milk and lemon juice into the creamed mixture. Whisk the egg whites in a grease-free mixing bowl until stiff and standing in peaks. Fold into the mixture using a metal spoon or rubber spatula.

Pour into the prepared dish and place in a baking tray filled with enough cold water to come halfway up the sides of the dish. Bake in the preheated oven for about 45 minutes, or until the sponge is firm and golden brown. Remove from the oven. Serve immediately with the custard or fresh cream.

Try this: FOR AN ALTERNATIVE: 314   FOR A MAIN COURSE: 202

Apple & Cinnamon Brown Betty

SERVES 4

450 g/1 lb cooking apples
50 g/2 oz caster sugar
finely grated rind of 1 lemon
125 g/4 oz fresh white
   breadcrumbs
125 g/4 oz demerara sugar

½ tsp ground cinnamon
25 g/1 oz butter

For the custard:
3 medium egg yolks
1 tbsp caster sugar

500 ml/1 pint milk
1 tbsp cornflour
few drops of vanilla essence

Preheat the oven to 180˚C/350˚F/Gas Mark 4. Lightly oil a 900 ml/1½ pint ovenproof dish.

Peel, core and slice the apples and place in a saucepan with the caster sugar, lemon rind and 2 tablespoons of water. Simmer for 10–15 minutes or until tender.

Mix the breadcrumbs with the sugar and the cinnamon. Place half the sweetened apples in the base of the prepared dish and spoon over half of the crumb mixture. Place the remaining apples on top and cover with the rest of the crumb mixture.

Melt the butter and pour over the surface of the pudding. Cover the dish with non-stick baking paper and bake in the preheated oven for 20 minutes. Remove the paper and bake for a further 10–15 minutes, or until golden.

Meanwhile, make the custard by whisking the egg yolks and sugar together until creamy. Mix 1 tablespoon of the milk with the cornflour until a paste forms and reserve.

Warm the rest of the milk until nearly boiling and pour over the egg mixture with the paste and vanilla essence. Place the bowl over a saucepan of gently simmering water. Stir over the heat until thickened and able to coat the back of a spoon. Strain into a jug and serve hot over the pudding.

Try this: FOR AN ALTERNATIVE: 306   FOR A MAIN COURSE: 138

Baked Apple Dumplings

SERVES 4

225 g/8 oz self-raising flour
¼ tsp salt
125 g/4 oz shredded suet

4 medium cooking apples
4–6 tsp luxury mincemeat
1 medium egg white, beaten

2 tsp caster sugar
custard or vanilla sauce,
  to serve

Preheat the oven to 200°C/400°F/Gas Mark 6. Lightly oil a baking tray. Place the flour and salt in a bowl and stir in the suet. Add just enough water to the mixture to mix to a soft but not sticky dough, using the fingertips.

Turn the dough on to a lightly floured board and knead lightly into a ball. Divide the dough into 4 pieces and roll out each piece into a thin square, large enough to encase the apples.

Peel and core the apples and place 1 apple in the centre of each square of pastry.

Fill the centre of the apple with mincemeat, brush the edges of each pastry square with water and draw the corners up to meet over each apple. Press the edges of the pastry firmly together and decorate with pastry leaves and shapes made from the extra pastry trimmings.

Place the apples on the prepared baking tray, brush with the egg white and sprinkle with the sugar.

Bake in the preheated oven for 30 minutes or until golden and the pastry and apples are cooked. Serve the dumplings hot with the custard or vanilla sauce.

Try this: FOR AN ALTERNATIVE: 314   FOR A MAIN COURSE: 128

Summer Pavlova

SERVES 6–8

4 medium egg whites
225 g/8 oz caster sugar
1 tsp vanilla essence
2 tsp white wine vinegar
1½ tsp cornflour

300 ml/½ pint half-fat
    Greek-set yogurt
2 tbsp honey
225 g/8 oz strawberries,
    hulled

125 g/4 oz raspberries
125 g/4 oz blueberries
4 kiwis, peeled and sliced
icing sugar, to decorate

Preheat the oven to 150°C/300°F/Gas Mark 2. Line a baking sheet with a sheet of greaseproof or baking parchment paper.

Place the egg whites in a clean grease-free bowl and whisk until very stiff. Whisk in half the sugar, vanilla essence, vinegar and cornflour, continue whisking until stiff. Gradually, whisk in the remaining sugar, a teaspoonful at a time until very stiff and glossy.

Using a large spoon, arrange spoonfuls of the meringue in a circle on the greaseproof paper or baking parchment paper. Bake in the preheated oven for 1 hour until crisp and dry. Turn the oven off and leave the meringue in the oven to cool completely.

Remove the meringue from the baking sheet and peel away the parchment paper. Mix together the yogurt and honey. Place the pavlova on a serving plate and spoon the yogurt into the centre.

Scatter over the strawberries, raspberries, blueberries and kiwis. Dust with the icing sugar and serve

Try this: FOR AN ALTERNATIVE: 310   FOR A MAIN COURSE: 290

Strawberry Flan

SERVES 4

For the sweet pastry:
175 g/6 oz plain flour
50 g/2 oz butter
50 g/2 oz white vegetable fat
2 tsp caster sugar
1 medium egg yolk, beaten

For the filling:
1 medium egg, plus 1 extra
    egg yolk
50 g/2 oz caster sugar
25 g/1 oz plain flour
300 ml/½ pint milk

few drops of vanilla essence
450 g/1 lb strawberries,
    cleaned and hulled
mint leaves, to decorate

Preheat the oven to 200°C/400°F/Gas Mark 6. Place the flour, butter and vegetable fat in a food processor and blend until the mixture resembles fine breadcrumbs. Stir in the sugar, then with the machine running, add the egg yolk and enough water to make a fairly stiff dough. Knead lightly, cover and chill in the refrigerator for 30 minutes.

Roll out the pastry and use to line a 23 cm/9 inch loose-bottomed flan tin. Place a piece of greaseproof paper in the pastry case and cover with baking beans or rice. Bake in the preheated oven for 15–20 minutes, until just firm. Reserve until cool.

Make the filling by whisking the eggs and sugar together until thick and pale. Gradually stir in the flour and then the milk. Pour into a small saucepan and simmer for 3–4 minutes stirring throughout.

Add the vanilla essence to taste, then pour into a bowl and leave to cool. Cover with greaseproof paper to prevent a skin from forming.

When the filling is cold, whisk until smooth then pour on to the cooked flan case. Slice the strawberries and arrange on the top of the filling. Decorate with the mint leaves and serve.

Try this: FOR AN ALTERNATIVE: 332   FOR A MAIN COURSE: 146

SERVES 6

Rich Double–crust Plum Pie

For the pastry:
75 g/3 oz butter
75 g/3 oz white vegetable fat
225 g/8 oz plain flour

2 medium egg yolks

For the filling:
450 g/1 lb fresh plums,

preferably Victoria
50 g/2 oz caster sugar
1 tbsp milk
a little extra caster sugar

Preheat the oven to 200°C/400°F/Gas Mark 6. Make the pastry by rubbing the butter and white vegetable fat into the flour until it resembles fine breadcrumbs or blend in a food processor. Add the egg yolks and enough water to make a soft dough. Knead lightly, then wrap and leave in the refrigerator for about 30 minutes.

Meanwhile, prepare the fruit. Rinse and dry the plums, then cut in half and remove the stones. Slice the plums into chunks and cook in a saucepan with 25 g/1 oz of the sugar and 2 tablespoons of water for 5–7 minutes, or until slightly softened. Remove from the heat and add the remaining sugar to taste and allow to cool.

Roll out half the chilled pastry on a lightly floured surface and use to line the base and sides of a 1.1 litre/ 2 pint pie dish. Allow the pastry to hang over the edge of the dish. Spoon in the prepared plums.

Roll out the remaining pastry to use as the lid and brush the edge with a little water. Wrap the pastry around the rolling pin and place over the plums. Press the edges together to seal and mark a decorative edge around the rim of the pastry by pinching with the thumb and forefinger or using the back of a fork. Brush the lid with milk, and make a few slits in the top. Use any trimmings to decorate the top of the pie with pastry leaves. Place on a baking sheet and bake in the preheated oven for 30 minutes, or until golden brown. Sprinkle with a little caster sugar and serve hot or cold.

Try this: FOR AN ALTERNATIVE: 324   FOR A MAIN COURSE: 178

Crunchy Rhubarb Crumble

SERVES 6

125 g/4 oz plain flour
50 g/2 oz softened butter
50 g/2 oz rolled oats

50 g/2 oz demerara sugar
1 tbsp sesame seeds
½ tsp ground cinnamon

450 g/1 lb fresh rhubarb
50 g/2 oz caster sugar
custard or cream, to serve

Preheat the oven to 180°C/350°F/Gas Mark 4. Place the flour in a large bowl and cut the butter into cubes. Add to the flour and rub in with the fingertips until the mixture looks like fine breadcrumbs, or blend for a few seconds in a food processor.

Stir in the rolled oats, demerara sugar, sesame seeds and cinnamon. Mix well and reserve.

Prepare the rhubarb by removing the thick ends of the stalks and cut diagonally into 2.5 cm/1 inch chunks. Wash thoroughly and pat dry with a clean tea towel. Place the rhubarb in a 1.1 litre/ 2 pint pie dish.

Sprinkle the caster sugar over the rhubarb and top with the reserved crumble mixture. Level the top of the crumble so that all the fruit is well covered and press down firmly. If liked, sprinkle the top with a little extra caster sugar.

Place on a baking sheet and bake in the preheated oven for 40–50 minutes, or until the fruit is soft and the topping is golden brown. Sprinkle the pudding with some more caster sugar and serve hot with custard or cream.

Try this: FOR AN ALTERNATIVE: 314   FOR A MAIN COURSE: 120

Crème Brûlée with Sugared Raspberries

SERVES 6

600 ml/1 pint fresh
   whipping cream
4 medium egg yolks

75 g/3 oz caster sugar
½ tsp vanilla essence
25 g/1 oz demerara sugar

175 g/6 oz fresh raspberries

Preheat the oven to 150°C/300°F/Gas Mark 2. Pour the cream into a bowl and place over a saucepan of gently simmering water. Heat gently but do not allow to boil.

Meanwhile, whisk together the egg yolks, 50 g/2 oz of the caster sugar and the vanilla essence. When the cream is warm, pour it over the egg mixture briskly whisking until it is mixed completely. Pour into 6 individual ramekin dishes and place in a roasting tin.

Fill the tin with sufficient water to come halfway up the sides of the dishes. Bake in the preheated oven for about 1 hour, or until the puddings are set. To test if set, carefully insert a round bladed knife into the centre, if the knife comes out clean they are set.

Remove the puddings from the roasting tin and allow to cool. Chill in the refrigerator, preferably overnight.

Sprinkle the sugar over the top of each dish and place the puddings under a preheated hot grill.

When the sugar has caramelised and turned deep brown, remove from the heat and cool. Chill the puddings in the refrigerator for 2–3 hours before serving.

Toss the raspberries in the remaining caster sugar and sprinkle over the top of each dish. Serve with a little extra cream if liked.

Try this: FOR AN ALTERNATIVE: 320   FOR A MAIN COURSE: 188

Jam Roly Poly

SERVES 6

225 g/8 oz self-raising flour
¼ tsp salt
125 g/4 oz shredded suet

about 150 ml/¼ pint water
3 tbsp strawberry jam
1 tbsp milk, to glaze

1 tsp caster sugar
ready-made jam sauce,
   to serve

Preheat the oven to 200°C/400°F/Gas Mark 6. Make the pastry by sifting the flour and salt into a large bowl. Add the suet and mix lightly, then add the water a little at a time and mix to form a soft and pliable dough. (Take care not to make the dough too wet.)

Turn the dough out on to a lightly floured board and knead gently until smooth. Roll the dough out into a 23 cm/9 inch x 28 cm/11 inch rectangle.

Spread the jam over the pastry leaving a border of 1 cm/½ inch all round. Fold the border over the jam and brush the edges with water.

Lightly roll the rectangle up from one of the short sides, seal the top edge and press the ends together. (Do not roll the pudding up too tightly.)

Turn the pudding upside down on to a large piece of greaseproof paper large enough to come halfway up the sides. (If using non-stick paper, then oil lightly.) Tie the ends of the paper, to make a boat-shaped paper case for the pudding to sit in and to leave plenty of room for the roly poly to expand.

Brush the pudding lightly with milk and sprinkle with the sugar. Bake in the preheated oven for 30–40 minutes, or until well risen and golden. Serve immediately with the jam sauce.

Try this: FOR AN ALTERNATIVE: 300   FOR A MAIN COURSE: 280

Iced Bakewell Tart

CUTS INTO 8 SLICES

For the rich pastry:
175 g/6 oz plain flour
pinch of salt
60 g/2½ oz butter, cut into
   small pieces
50 g/2 oz white vegetable
   fat, cut into small pieces
2 small egg yolks, beaten

For the filling:
125 g/4 oz butter, melted
125 g/4 oz caster sugar
125 g/4 oz ground almonds
2 large eggs, beaten
few drops of almond
   essence
2 tbsp seedless raspberry jam

For the icing:
125 g/4 oz icing sugar, sifted
6–8 tsp fresh lemon juice
25 g/1 oz toasted flaked
   almonds

Preheat the oven to 200°C/400°F/Gas Mark 6. Place the flour and salt in a bowl, rub in the butter and vegetable fat until the mixture resembles breadcrumbs. Alternatively, blend quickly, in short bursts in a food processor.

Add the eggs with sufficient water to make a soft, pliable dough. Knead lightly on a floured board then chill in the refrigerator for about 30 minutes. Roll out the pastry and use to line a 23 cm/9 inch loose-bottomed flan tin.

For the filling, mix together the melted butter, sugar, almonds and beaten eggs and add a few drops of almond essence. Spread the base of the pastry case with the raspberry jam and spoon over the egg mixture. Bake in the preheated oven for about 30 minutes, or until the filling is firm and golden brown. Remove from the oven and allow to cool completely.

When the tart is cold make the icing by mixing together the icing sugar and lemon juice, a little at a time, until the icing is smooth and of a spreadable consistency.

Spread the icing over the tart, leave to set for 2–3 minutes and sprinkle with the almonds. Chill in the refrigerator for about 10 minutes and serve.

Try this: FOR AN ALTERNATIVE: 320   FOR A MAIN COURSE: 94

Egg Custard Tart

SERVES 6

For the sweet pastry:
50 g/2 oz butter
50 g/2 oz white vegetable fat
175 g/6 oz plain flour
1 medium egg yolk, beaten

2 tsp caster sugar

For the filling:
300 ml/½ pint milk
2 medium eggs, plus

1 medium egg yolk
25 g/1 oz caster sugar
½ tsp freshly grated nutmeg

Preheat the oven to 200˚C/400˚F/Gas Mark 6. Oil a 20.5 cm/8 inch flan tin or dish.

Make the pastry by cutting the butter and vegetable fat into small cubes. Add to the flour in a large bowl and rub in, until the mixture resembles fine breadcrumbs. Add the egg, sugar and enough water to form a soft and pliable dough. Turn on to a lightly floured board and knead. Wrap and chill in the refrigerator for 30 minutes.

Roll the pastry out on to a lightly floured surface or pastry board and use to line the oiled flan tin. Place in the refrigerator to reserve.

Warm the milk in a small saucepan. Briskly whisk together the eggs, egg yolk and caster sugar. Pour the milk into the egg mixture and whisk until blended. Strain through a sieve into the pastry case. Place the flan tin on a baking sheet.

Sprinkle the top of the tart with nutmeg and bake in the preheated oven for about 15 minutes.

Turn the oven down to 170˚C/325˚F/Gas Mark 3 and bake for a further 30 minutes, or until the custard has set. Serve hot or cold.

Try this: FOR AN ALTERNATIVE: 320   FOR A MAIN COURSE: 182

Lattice Treacle Tart

SERVES 4

For the pastry:
175 g/6 oz plain flour
40 g/1½ oz butter
40 g/1½ oz white vegetable fat

For the filling:
225 g/8 oz golden syrup
finely grated rind and juice
  of 1 lemon

75 g/3 oz fresh white
  breadcrumbs
1 small egg, beaten

Preheat the oven to 190°C/375°F/Gas Mark 5.

Make the pastry by placing the flour, butter and white vegetable fat in a food processor. Blend in short, sharp bursts until the mixture resembles fine breadcrumbs. Remove from the processor and place on a pastry board or in a large bowl. Stir in enough cold water to make a dough and knead in a large bowl or on a floured surface until smooth and pliable.

Roll out the pastry and use to line a 20.5 cm/8 inch loose-bottomed fluted flan tin. Reserve the pastry trimmings for decoration and chill for 30 minutes.

Meanwhile, to make the filling, place the golden syrup in a saucepan and warm gently with the lemon rind and juice. Tip the breadcrumbs into the pastry case and pour the syrup mixture over the top.

Roll the pastry trimmings out on a lightly floured surface and cut into 6–8 thin strips. Lightly dampen the pastry edge of the tart, then place the strips across the filling in a lattice pattern. Brush the ends of the strips with water and seal to the edge of the tart. Brush a little beaten egg over the pastry and bake in the preheated oven for a 25 minutes, or until the filling is just set. Serve hot or cold.

Try this: FOR AN ALTERNATIVE: 302 FOR A MAIN COURSE: 204

Chocolate Chip Ice Cream

SERVES 4

350 g/12 oz fresh raspberries, or thawed if frozen	600 ml/1 pint milk	450 g/1 lb plain dark chocolate
25 g/1 oz icing sugar, or to taste	1 vanilla pod, seeds removed	150 ml/¼ pint double cream
2 tbsp lemon juice	6 medium egg yolks	fresh fruit of your choice, to serve
	125 g/4 oz caster sugar	

Set the freezer to rapid freeze. Simmer the raspberries with the sugar and lemon juice for 5 minutes. Leave to cool, then purée in a food processor. Press through a fine sieve to remove the pips. Reserve the coulis.

Pour the milk into a heavy-based saucepan and add the vanilla pod. Bring slowly to the boil, then remove from the heat and leave to infuse for 30 minutes. Remove the pod. Whisk the egg yolks and caster sugar together until pale and creamy, then gradually whisk in the infused milk. Strain the mixture into a clean saucepan, place over a gentle heat and bring slowly to the boil. Cook over a gentle heat, stirring constantly, until the mixture thickens and coats the back of a wooden spoon. Do not let the mixture boil otherwise it will curdle. Once thickened, cover with clingfilm and leave the custard to cool completely.

Break half the chocolate into small pieces and place in a heatproof bowl set over a saucepan of gently simmering water. Heat gently, stirring frequently, until the chocolate has melted and smooth. Remove from the heat and leave to cool. Whip the cream until soft peaks form and fold into the cooled custard. Roughly chop the remaining chocolate and stir into the custard mixture together with the melted chocolate. Spoon into a suitable container and freeze for 1 hour. Remove from the freezer and beat well to break up all the ice crystals. Repeat the beating and freezing process twice more, then freeze for 4 hours or until the ice cream is solid. Allow to soften in the refrigerator for 30 minutes before serving with fresh fruit and the raspberry coulis. Remember to return the freezer to its normal setting.

Chocolate Mousse

SERVES 6

175 g/6 oz milk or plain
  chocolate orange
535 g carton ready-
  made custard

450 ml/¾ pint
  double cream
12 Cape gooseberries,
  to decorate

sweet biscuits,
  to serve

Break the chocolate into segments and place in a bowl set over a saucepan of simmering water. Leave until melted, stirring occasionally. Remove the bowl in the pan from the heat and allow the melted chocolate to cool slightly.

Place the custard in a bowl and fold the melted chocolate into it using a metal spoon or rubber spatula. Stir well until completely combined.

Pour the cream into a small bowl and whip until the cream forms soft peaks. Using a metal spoon or rubber spatula fold in most of the whipped cream into the chocolate mixture.

Spoon into six tall glasses and carefully top with the remaining cream.

Leave the desserts to chill in the refrigerator for at least 1 hour or preferably overnight.

Peel back the skins from the gooseberries to form petal shapes and use to decorate the chocolate desserts. Serve with the sweet biscuits.

Try this: FOR AN ALTERNATIVE: 344   FOR A MAIN COURSE: 244

Chocolate Fudge Sundae

SERVES 2

**For the chocolate
    fudge sauce:**
75 g/3 oz plain dark
    chocolate, broken
    into pieces
450ml/¾ pint double cream
175g/6 oz golden
    caster sugar

25 g/1 oz plain flour
pinch of salt
15 g/½ oz unsalted butter
1 tsp vanilla essence

For the sundae:
125 g/4 oz raspberries, fresh
    or thawed if frozen

4 scoops vanilla ice cream
2 scoops chocolate
    ice cream
2 tbsp toasted flaked
    almonds
a few wafers,
    to serve

To make the chocolate fudge sauce, place the chocolate and cream in a heavy-based saucepan and heat gently until the chocolate has melted into the cream. Stir until smooth. Mix the sugar with the flour and salt, then stir in sufficient chocolate mixture to make a smooth paste.

Gradually blend the remaining melted chocolate mixture into the paste, then pour into a clean saucepan. Cook over a low heat, stirring frequently until smooth and thick. Remove from the heat and add the butter and vanilla essence. Stir until smooth, then cool slightly.

To make the sundae, crush the raspberries lightly with a fork and reserve. Spoon a little of the chocolate sauce into the bottom of two sundae glasses. Add a layer of crushed raspberries, then a scoop each of vanilla and chocolate ice cream.

Top each one with a scoop of the vanilla ice cream. Pour over the sauce, sprinkle over the almonds and serve with a wafer.

Try this: FOR AN ALTERNATIVE: 336   FOR A MAIN COURSE: 200

Black Forest Gateau

CUTS 10–12 SLICES

250 g/9 oz butter
1 tbsp instant coffee granules
350 ml/12 fl oz hot water
200 g/7 oz plain dark
    chocolate, chopped or
    broken

400 g/14 oz caster sugar
225 g/8 oz self-raising flour
150 g/5 oz plain flour
50 g/2 oz cocoa powder
2 medium eggs
2 tsp vanilla essence

2 x 400 g cans stoned
    cherries in juice
2 tsp arrowroot
600 ml/1 pint double cream
50 ml/2 fl oz kirsch

Preheat the oven to 150˚C/300˚F/Gas Mark 2, 5 minutes before serving. Lightly oil and line a deep 23 cm/9 inch cake tin.

Melt the butter in a large saucepan. Blend the coffee with the hot water, add to the butter with the chocolate and sugar and heat gently, stirring until smooth. Pour into a large bowl and leave until just warm. Sift together the flours and cocoa powder. Using an electric mixer, whisk the warm chocolate mixture on a low speed, then gradually whisk in the dry ingredients. Whisk in the eggs 1 at a time, then the vanilla essence. Pour the mixture into the prepared tin and bake in the preheated oven for 1 hour 45 minutes or until firm and a skewer inserted into the centre comes out clean. Leave in the tin for 5 minutes to cool slightly before turning out onto a wire rack.

Place the cherries and their juice in a small saucepan and heat gently. Blend the arrowroot with 2 teaspoons of water until smooth, then stir into the cherries. Cook, stirring, until the liquid thickens. Simmer very gently for 2 minutes, then leave until cold.

Whisk the double cream until thick. Trim the top of the cake if necessary, then split the cake into 3 layers. Brush the base of the cake with half the kirsch. Top with a layer of cream and one-third of the cherries. Repeat the layering, then place the third layer on top. Reserve a little cream for decorating and use the remainder to cover the top and sides of the cake. Pipe a decorative edge around the cake, then arrange the remaining cherries in the centre and serve.

Try this: FOR AN ALTERNATIVE: 344   FOR A MAIN COURSE: 100

Individual Steamed Chocolate Puddings

SERVES 4

150 g/5 oz unsalted
  butter, softened
175 g/6 oz light
  muscovado sugar
½ tsp freshly grated nutmeg

25 g/1 oz plain white flour, sifted
4 tbsp cocoa powder, sifted
5 medium eggs, separated
125 g/4 oz ground almonds
50 g/2 oz white breadcrumbs

To serve:
Greek yogurt
orange-flavoured
  chocolate curls

Preheat the oven to 180°C/350°F/Gas Mark 4, 10 minutes before baking. Lightly oil and line the bases of eight individual 175 ml/6 fl oz pudding basins with a small circle of non-stick baking parchment.

Cream the butter with 50 g/2 oz of the sugar and the nutmeg until light and fluffy. Sift the flour and cocoa powder together, then stir into the creamed mixture. Beat in the egg yolks and mix well, then fold in the ground almonds and the breadcrumbs.

Whisk the egg whites in a clean, grease-free bowl until stiff and standing in peaks then gradually whisk in the remaining sugar. Using a metal spoon, fold a quarter of the egg whites into the chocolate mixture and mix well, then fold in the remaining egg whites.

Spoon the mixture into the prepared basins, filling them two thirds full to allow for expansion. Cover with a double sheet of tinfoil and secure tightly with string. Stand the pudding basins in a roasting tin and pour in sufficient water to come halfway up the sides of the basins.

Bake in the centre of the preheated oven for 30 minutes, or until the puddings are firm to the touch. Remove from the oven, loosen around the edges and invert onto warmed serving plates. Serve immediately with Greek yogurt and chocolate curls.

Try this: FOR AN ALTERNATIVE: 342   FOR A MAIN COURSE: 278

Traditional Oven Scones

SERVES 4

225 g/8 oz self-raising flour
1 tsp baking powder
pinch of salt
40 g/1½ oz butter, cubed
15 g/½ oz caster sugar

150 ml/¼ pint milk, plus
1 tbsp for brushing
1 tbsp plain flour, to dust

**For a lemon and sultana
scone variation:**
50 g/2 oz sultanas
finely grated rind of ½ lemon
beaten egg, to glaze

Preheat the oven to 220˚C/425˚F/Gas Mark 7, 15 minutes before baking. Sift the flour, baking powder and salt into a large bowl. Rub in the butter until the mixture resembles fine breadcrumbs. Stir in the sugar and mix in enough milk to give a fairly soft dough.

Knead the dough on a lightly floured surface for a few seconds until smooth. Roll out until 2 cm/¾ inches thick and stamp out 6.5 cm/2½ inch rounds with a floured plain cutter.

Place on an oiled baking sheet and brush the tops with milk (do not brush it over the sides or the scones will not rise properly). Dust with a little plain flour.

Bake in the preheated oven for 12–15 minutes, or until well risen and golden brown. Transfer to a wire rack and serve warm or leave to cool completely. (The scones are best eaten on the day of baking but may be kept in an airtight tin for up to 2 days.)

For lemon and sultana scones, stir in the sultanas and lemon rind with the sugar. Roll out until 2 cm/¾ inches thick and cut into 8 fingers, 10 x 2.5 cm/4 x 1 inch in size. Bake the scones as before.

Try this: FOR AN ALTERNATIVE: 348   FOR A MAIN COURSE: 92

Scottish Shortbread

SERVES 4

225 g/8 oz plain flour
60 g/2 oz rice flour
¼ tsp salt
175 g/6 oz unsalted butter, at

room temperature
60 g/2 oz caster sugar
25 g/1 oz icing sugar, sifted
¼ tsp vanilla essence

(extract) (optional)
sugar, for sprinkling

Lightly grease two 20–23 cm/8–9 inch cake or tart tins with removable bases. Sift the plain flour, rice flour and salt into a bowl and set aside.

Using an electric mixer, beat the butter for about 1 minute in a large bowl until creamy. Add the sugars and continue beating for 1–2 minutes until very light and fluffy. If using, beat in the vanilla.

Using a wooden spoon, stir the flour mixture into the butter and sugar until well blended. Turn onto a lightly floured surface and knead lightly to blend completely.

Divide the dough evenly between the 2 tins, smoothing the surface. Using a fork, press 2 cm/ ¾ inch radiating lines around the edge of the dough. Lightly sprinkle the surfaces with a little sugar, then prick the surface lightly with the fork.

Using a sharp knife, mark each dough round into 8 wedges. Bake in a preheated oven at 120°C/250°F/Gas Mark ½ for 50–60 minutes until pale golden and crisp. Cool in the tins on a wire rack for about 5 minutes.

Carefully remove the side of each pan and slide the bottoms onto a heatproof surface. Using the knife marks as a guide, cut each shortbread into 8 wedges while still warm. Cool completely on the wire rack, then store in airtight containers.

Try this: FOR AN ALTERNATIVE: 346   FOR A MAIN COURSE: 122

Index